京都国立近代美術館所蔵作品にみる
From MoMAK Collection

京（みやこ）のくらし
二十四節気を愉しむ

Life in Kyoto
Arts in Seasonal Delight

編著　京都国立近代美術館 ＋ 筧 菜奈子
Edited by The National Museum of Modern Art, Kyoto + KAKEI Nanako

青幻舎

はじめに

日本には、はっきりとした四季の変化があります。また、春夏秋冬の四つの季節の中にも、様々な変化があることには皆さんもお気づきのことでしょう。そうした細やかな季節の変化を捉えた暦が二十四節気と七十二候です。それぞれ一年を二十四等分、あるいは七十二等分にしたもので、気候や動植物の様子が季節名としてつけられているのが特徴です。

もっとも細やかな七十二候に従えば、季節は約五日ごとに移り変わっていきます。とはいえ忙しない日々の中で、この繊細な移り変わりを意識することはなかなか難しいものです。ですが、この春は季節の移ろいをじっくりと感じ取ることができました。というのもコロナウイルスによる自粛生活の中で散歩が日課となり、道端の花が日ごとに開いていく様子や、樹々が緑を深めていく様子を観察することができたからです。鬱々とした状況下ではありましたが、季節の変化を感じながら生活できたことは、贅沢な喜びとなりました。

さて、私たちの生活がそうであるように、芸術作品も季節と無関係には存在できません。本書は、京都にゆかりのある作家たちを中心に取りあげ、その四季にまつわる作品を紹介するものです。作品をみれば、絵画の主題として、あるいは着物や工芸品の文様として季節が表現されていることがわかるでしょう。また、季節を主題としない作品であっても、どこかしら季節が滲み出ている点にも注目してみてください。

私は学生の頃、八年ほど京都に住んでいました。違う土地に移った今でも、ふとした瞬間に京都で過ごした日々が頭をよぎります。鴨川沿いに咲く枝垂桜の色や、祇園祭前の四条通りの緊張感、街を囲む山々の紅葉、冬の寺社の床板の冷たさ……思い返してみれば、京都で過ごした日々は、季節と一体となって記憶されていることに気づきます。そして、毎年同じ季節が繰り返されているようで、一つとして同じ季節はなかったことにも。

芸術作品を通して季節を感じる喜びは、実はこの「同じ季節は二度訪れない」というところにあるのではないかと思います。本書に並ぶ作品の多くは、作家が実際に目にしていた京都の情景をもとに制作されたものです。当然、私たちは作家たちが過ごした季節を体感することは出来ません。しかし、残された芸術作品から、その季節が確かに存在していたことを感じることはできます。芸術家の目を介した京都の四季折々を、ぜひじっくりと味わってみてください。

筧　菜奈子

KAKEI Nanako

In Japan we have four distinct seasons—spring, summer, autumn, winter. You may also be aware that there are variations within the four seasons. In the old calendar that took into account those subtle seasonal changes, the seasons are divided into a subset of twenty-four seasonal periods and further into seventy-two seasonal stages. These carve the year into twenty-four and seventy-two segments, respectively, identified by seasonal nomenclature that reflects the weather or the state of flora and fauna.

The most detailed classification into seventy-two segments indicates a shift in seasons every five days or so. That said, it is quite difficult for us to be aware of these slight transitions as we go about our busy days. However, this spring I was able to pay attention to the variations within the season. Under the stay at home stricture due to the coronavirus, on my daily walks I could observe how the street-side flowers began to bloom and the deepening of the greenery of the trees along my route. Within these dispiriting circumstances, being able to spend my days while feeling the shifts within the season was a luxury I enjoyed.

Just as our lives are affected by the seasons, artworks cannot exist without relation to the seasons. This volume introduces works connected to the twenty-four seasonal periods with a focus on artists with deep ties to Kyoto. Looking at the works, we can see the season expressed in the subject of a painting or the design of a kimono or craftwork. Be sure to note that even those works that are not specifically about a season can exude seasonality.

I lived in Kyoto for eight years or so while I was a student. Although I have moved elsewhere, at odd moments, the days I spent in Kyoto still flit across my mind. The color of the weeping cherry blossoms along the Kamo River, the excitement along Shijo street leading up to the Gion Festival, the fall colors that envelop the city, the chill of the wooden floors of temples and shrines in winter—I realize that my memories of the years I spent in Kyoto are fused with the seasons. I also recognize that each year the same seasons seem to recur, but none is exactly the same as in other years.

The pleasure we feel in sensing the seasons through artworks may actually be because "no two seasons are alike." Many of the art objects in this volume are produced from the scenes of Kyoto that the artists saw with their own eyes. It goes without saying that we cannot experience the same season that the artists did in the past. But from the artworks they have left to us we can sense for certain the existence of the seasons they depicted. Please take the time to savor the seasonal occasions of Kyoto as presented through the eyes of these artists.

目次 | Index

初春

旧暦一月・新暦二月・睦月

《立春》　新暦二月四日頃
春が生まれる

《雨水》　新暦二月十八日頃
草木が芽吹く

まだ寒さが身に沁みる二月の始め、暦の上では「立春」。いよいよ春が始まります。神阪松濤の《椿》には、霞にけぶる椿が丹念な筆致で描かれています。次々とひらいていく淡紅色の花のいただきには一羽の鶯が。美しい鳴き声から「春告鳥」とも呼ばれる鳥ですが、今はそろそろと鳴き声の練習を始めているところかもしれません。

雪が雨へと変わる二月末ごろ、大地がゆるみ、草木が萌え始めます。さらに寒さを吹き飛ばすのが、この時期に南から吹く「春一番」。この風にほぐされるかのように梅が次々と蕾をひらかせます。京都にはさまざまな梅の名所がありますが、一度は目にしたいのが、尾形光琳の梅図のモデルになったともいわれる下鴨神社の「光琳の梅」。黒ずんだ枝々から、紅梅が燃え上がるように爛爛と咲きます。梅に続いて、マンサク、サンシュユ、カタクリ、桃と花が次々と咲き出して、春が一挙になだれ込んでくるようです。

EARLY SPRING

1st Month under Japanese lunisolar calendar | February | *MUTSUKI*

RISSHUN
[Beginning of Spring]

February 4th
Spring is awaking.

USUI
[Rainwater]

February 18th
Grass and trees are sprouting.

Though the cold still chills the body in early February, the ancient calendar notes the Beginning of Spring. Spring is about to come at last. Kamisaka Shoto's *Camellias* depicts with deft brushstrokes a camellia bush showing dimly through the haze. A bush warbler alights on the top branch of the bush of light pink blossoms. Its beautiful song gives it the moniker "bird that announces spring," and it may be practicing its song about now.

Toward the end of February, when the snow turns to rain, the earth softens and grasses and trees begin to bud. What blows away the chill is the first strong south winds of the year. Plum blossoms unfurl as if loosened by this wind. There are myriad famed spots for plum blossoms in Kyoto, but at least once one should see Shimogamo Shrine's "Korin's Plum" that is said to be the model for Ogata Korin's plum blossom painting. From blackened branches red plum blossoms bloom with a fiery brilliance. Next come blossoms of Japanese witch hazel, Japanese cornel dogwood, dogtooth violet, and peach, one after another as spring rushes forward.

椿｜神阪松濤
Camellias｜KAMISAKA Shoto

初春｜EARLY SPRING

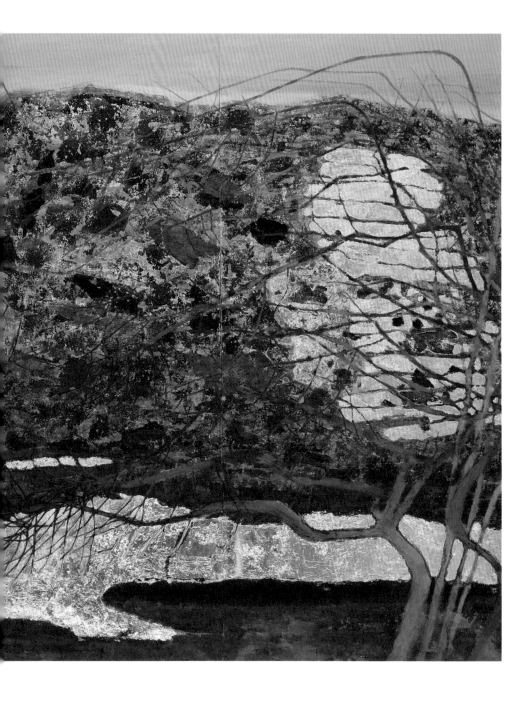

残雪とは、冬に積もった雪が春になっても消えないで
残っていることを言います。複雑に折れ伸びる枯れ木の
合間から、焦茶色の山肌と土混じりの残雪がのぞいてい
ます。日本画家として活躍していた秋野不矩は、1962
年のインド訪問を契機にその画風を大きく変革させま
した。光にあふれる雄大な自然を鮮烈に描き出すその表
現は、日本画の世界に新風を吹き込んでいます。

Melting snow refers to the snow that is still left from the
accumulation of winter even after spring has arrived. The burnt
brown of the mountainside and the leftover snow mixed with earth
peak through the tangle of broken and withered trees. Having been
active as a Japanese-style painter, Akino Fuku made a major change
in his style after his trip to India in 1962. His expression of vivid
depictions of the grandeur of nature bathed in light blew a new
wind into the world of Japanese-style painting.

残雪 ｜ 秋野不矩 ｜ 昭和55 ｜ 紙本、着色、額
Melting Snow ｜ AKINO Fuku ｜ 1980 ｜ color on paper, framed

1

2

1　二尊院春雪｜伊藤仁三郎｜昭和35-44｜紙、木版
Spring Snow in Nison-in Temple｜ITO Nisaburo｜1960-69｜paper, woodblock print

2　羽衣蒔絵料紙硯箱｜八世 西村彦兵衛（象彦）｜明治末〜昭和初｜木・漆・金、蒔絵
Writing Paper Box and Inkstone Box with Hagoromo (Robe of Feathers) Design, Maki-e｜NISHIMURA Hikobei VIII (Zohiko)｜
c. 1910-30｜wood, lacquer, gold, maki-e

1

3

2

1　**春雪**｜竹内栖鳳｜昭和17｜絹本、着色、額
　Spring Snow｜TAKEUCHI Seiho｜1942｜color on silk, framed

2　**象嵌彩窯変春うらら花壷**｜今井政之｜平成2｜陶器・釉薬、象嵌
　Flower Vase with Inlay Decoration: Glorious Spring｜IMAI Masayuki｜1990｜ceramic, glaze, inlay

3　**椿小禽図花瓶**｜海野勝珉｜明治時代｜銀、象嵌（金・赤銅・四分一）
　Vase with Birds and Camellias Design｜UNNO Shomin｜1868-1912｜silver, inlay (gold, shakudo, shibuichi copper alloy)

1

2

1　**椿**｜神阪松濤｜明治末｜絹本、着色、額
Camellias｜KAMISAKA Shoto｜c. 1900-12｜color on silk, framed

2　**色絵椿模様飾箱（染付色絵椿之図飾筥）**｜富本憲吉｜昭和16｜磁器・釉薬、色絵
Casket with Camellias Design, Overglaze Enamels｜TOMIMOTO Kenkichi｜1941｜porcelain, glaze, overglaze enamels

1

3

2

1 鮭｜土田麦僊｜大正14｜絹本、着色、軸
Dish of Salmon｜TSUCHIDA Bakusen｜1924｜color on silk, hanging scroll

2 色絵金彩椿文鉢｜北大路魯山人｜昭和30｜陶器・釉薬、色絵・金彩
Bowl with Camellias Design, Overglaze Enamels and Gold｜KITAOJI Rosanjin｜1955｜ceramic, glaze, overglaze enamels, gold paint

3 緑釉窯変赤黒花瓶｜森野嘉光｜昭和42｜陶器・釉薬
Green Glaze Flower Vase, Red-Black Yohen (Pyrolyzed) Style｜MORINO Kako｜1967｜ceramic, glaze

訪問着「透流」｜小倉建亮｜昭和37｜絹・金糸・金箔、絞染・刺繍
Kimono: Clear Water｜OGURA Kensuke｜1962｜silk, gold thread, gold leaf, tie dyed, embroidery

1

2

1 **梅咲く早春** ｜ 河津光峻 ｜ 昭和10年代 ｜ 紙本、着色、額
   Early Spring in Plum Orchard ｜ KAWAZU Koshun ｜ 1935–45 ｜ color on paper, framed

2 **春風の扉ひらけば南無阿弥陀仏　山頭火** ｜ 池田遥邨 ｜ 昭和63 ｜ 紙本、着色、額
   "The Spring Breeze, Opens the Door, Namu Amida Butsu." by Santoka ｜ IKEDA Yoson ｜ 1988 ｜ color on paper, framed

1

3

2

1 **梅之図花瓶**｜林谷五郎｜大正時代｜金属・釉薬、有線七宝（一対）
Flower Vase with Plum Blossoms Design｜HAYASHITANI Goro｜1912-26｜metal, glaze, wired cloisonné, pair of flower vases

2 **染付梅花大飾皿**｜近藤悠三｜昭和50｜磁器・釉薬、染付
Large Ornamental Dish with Plum Blossoms Design, Blue and White｜KONDO Yuzo｜1975｜porcelain, glaze, blue underglaze

3 **白梅**｜猪原大華｜昭和39｜紙本、着色、額
White Plum Blossoms｜INOHARA Taika｜1964｜color on paper, framed

森口華弘は友禅染の作家です。京友禅の作品は華やかな色彩のものが多いですが、森口はあえて色数を抑えて、構図の妙で魅せる典雅な作品を発表しました。その卓越した技術は、重要無形文化財保持者に認定されるほどです。本作品は、春霞を思わせる薄紅色の点模様と、梅模様が斜めに反復される斬新な構図です。染めと刺繍とが巧みに組み合わせられているのも特徴で、金糸・銀糸の刺繍による花びらが煌びやかさを放ちます。

Moriguchi Kako was a yuzen-dye artist. While Kyo-yuzen tends toward works that are brightly colored, Moriguchi has intentionally limited the number of colors he used to focus on works that show refinement through his talent for design. His superb technique garnered him certification as a holder of Important Intangible Cultural Property, or Living National Treasure. In this work, he employs a novel design of the dotted pattern in light pink reminiscent of spring haze and the repetitive diagonal pattern of plum blossoms. Another feature is the skillful combination of dyeing and embroidery, with the gold and silver threads of embroidery adding a brilliance to the flower petals.

乾漆梅花盆 ｜ 黒田辰秋 ｜ 昭和41 ｜ 木・漆、乾漆
Plum Blossom Shaped Tray, Dry Lacquer ｜ KURODA Tatsuaki ｜ 1966 ｜ wood, lacquer, dry lacquer

振袖「梅林」｜森口華弘｜昭和39｜縮緬、友禅
Long-sleeved Kimono: Plum Orchard｜MORIGUCHI Kako｜1964｜silk crêpe, yuzen dyed

1

3

2

1　**城南早春**｜川端弥之助｜昭和14｜画布、油彩、額
　Early Spring in the South Suburb of Kyoto｜KAWABATA Yanosuke｜1939｜oil on canvas, framed

2　**芽**｜八木一夫｜昭和39｜陶器
　Bud｜YAGI Kazuo｜1964｜ceramic

3　**飾筥「早春」**｜藤田喬平｜昭和64｜ガラス
　Decorative Box: Early Spring｜FUJITA Kyohei｜1984｜glass

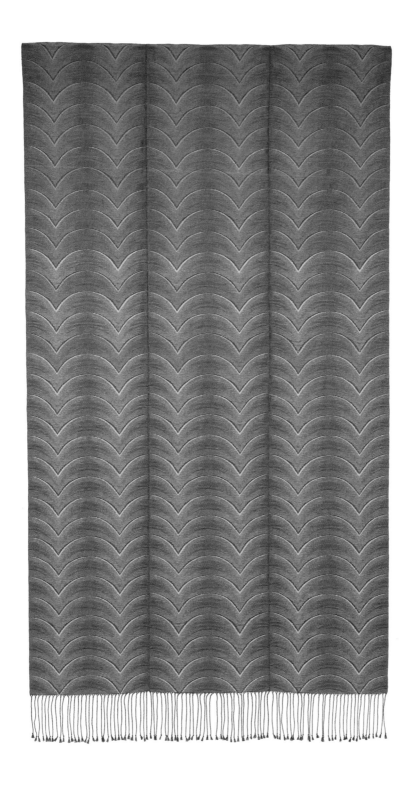

タペストリー「艸々」｜北村武資｜昭和53｜絹、変織
Tapestry: Spring Growing Grass　│ KITAMURA Takeshi　│ 1978 │ silk, unique waeving

仲春 旧暦二月・新暦三月・如月

《啓蟄》　新暦三月五日頃

　　　　　虫が這い出す

《春分》　新暦三月二十日頃

　　　　　昼と夜の時間が等しい

すっかり暖かくなり、冬ごもりをしていた虫や蛙がもぞもぞと動き出す季節。春うらら かという言葉がぴったりとあてはまるような明るく温かな日がある一方で、天気が大きく 崩れる日も多くあります。崩れた空にすら趣が感じられる季節で、「花曇」「春雨」「春雷」 など風雅な言葉が生み出されてきました。

春に羽化して麗しい姿を見せてくれるのが蝶々。「胡蝶の夢」をはじめとして、世界に は蝶と夢とを関連づける説話が多くあります。春のめざめはじめに、目の前をひらひらと 飛ぶ眩惑的な姿が、夢とも現ともわからぬ光景に感じられるのかもしれません。並河靖之 《桜蝶図平皿》には春を謳歌するように舞い飛ぶ蝶が、大小様々に描きとめられています。

周りを囲むのは可憐な八重桜。京都で桜がひらくのは、太陽が真東から出て真西に入る春 分のころです。京都御所の近衛桜を先がけとして、平野神社や鴨川沿岸の桜などが咲き揃 い、京都の街は一面淡いピンク色で染められます。

MID-SPRING

2nd Month under Japanese lunisolar calendar | March | *KISARAGI*

KEICHITSU
[Insects Awaken]

March 5th
Hibernating insects are surfacing.

SHUNBUN
[Spring Equinox]

March 20th
Length of night and day are equal.

As the season becomes warm, insects and frogs that were hibernating during the winter begin to move around. While clear and warm days of glorious weather become common, there are many days when the weather turns foul. In this season, there is elegance even in the sky when the weather becomes turbulent, described by evocative words like "flower cloudiness," "spring rain," and "spring thunder."

In spring, butterflies emerge in all their beauty. Throughout the world there are many tales relating butterflies to dreams, as does the Chinese "The Butterfly Dream." It may be that the dazzling flight of butterflies flitting into one's view as spring awakens makes one wonder whether that scene is a dream or reality. Namikawa Yasuyuki's *Plate with Cherry Blossoms and Butterflies Design* depicts large and small butterflies flying about, as if rejoicing in the season. Lovely double-blossomed cherries skirt the rim of the plate. In Kyoto cherry blossoms bloom around the spring equinox when the sun rises from due east and sets due west. Starting with the Konoye cherry blossoms in the Kyoto Imperial Palace, then with those in Hirano Shrine and along the Kamo River, the city becomes blanketed by light pink.

桜蝶図平皿 | 並河靖之
Plate with Cherry Blossoms and Butterflies Design | NAMIKAWA Yasuyuki

水中落花蝶図 ｜ 久保田米僊 ｜
明治中期 ｜ 絹本、着色、軸
Floating Flowers and Butterflies ｜
KUBOTA Beisen ｜
1875-95 ｜ color on silk, hanging scroll

3

1

2

1 **彩埏春花瓶**｜楠部彌弌｜昭和55｜磁器・釉薬
Flower Vase with Mulan Magnolia Design in Spring, Saien Technique｜KUSUBE Yaichi｜1980｜porcelain, glaze

2 **蜥蜴文硯箱**｜山脇洋二｜昭和22｜銀、鍛造・彫金
Inkstone Box with Lizard Design｜YAMAWAKI Yoji｜1947｜silver, wrought, carved

3 **遅日**｜野長瀬晩花｜大正9頃｜絹本、着色、軸
Long Spring Day｜NONAGASE Banka｜c. 1920｜color on silk, hanging scroll

蝶の中には同じルートを繰り返し飛ぶ種がいて、その通り道を「蝶道」と呼びます。本作の星図のような直線と、ゆったりとした8の字は、そうした道を表しているのかもしれません。作者の長谷川三郎は昭和の初めに、ヨーロッパやアメリカで最前衛の抽象絵画を学びました。帰国後は、東洋の書や禅に基づきながら、日本における抽象表現を開拓。イサム・ノグチと親交を結び、共に日本の前衛美術を大きくリードしました。

Some butterflies retrace the same pattern in their flight, and we call this route "butterfly way." This work seems to show this pattern in its constellation-like straight lines and loose figure-eight line. In the early 1930s, Hasegawa studied avant-garde painting in Europe and America. Upon his return to Japan he broke new ground in abstract art on the foundations of Eastern calligraphy and Zen. In association with Isamu Noguchi, he was a major figure of avant-garde art in Japan.

蝶の軌跡｜長谷川三郎｜昭和12｜画布、油彩、額
Locus of a Butterfly｜HASEGAWA Saburo｜1937｜oil on canvas, framed

1

3

2

1 **チューリップ** ｜ 足立源一郎 ｜ 大正6／9 ｜ 画布、油彩、額
　Tulips ｜ ADACHI Gen'ichiro ｜ 1917/20 ｜ oil on canvas, framed

2 **チューリップと三蝶** ｜ 長谷川 潔 ｜ 昭和35 ｜ 紙、マニエール・ノワール
　Tulip and Three Butterflies ｜ HASEGAWA Kiyoshi ｜ 1960 ｜ paper, manière noire

3 **チューリップ** ｜ 野島康三 ｜ 昭和15 ｜ ゼラチン・シルバー・プリント
　Tulips ｜ NOJIMA Yasuzo ｜ 1940 ｜ gelatin silver print

2

3

1

1 観音之図（聖蓮華）｜村上華岳｜昭和5｜紙本、淡彩、軸
Avalokitesvara (The Sacred Lotus)｜MURAKAMI Kagaku｜
1930｜light color on paper, hanging scroll

2 黄地紅彩龍雲文角皿｜加藤土師萌｜昭和28｜磁器・釉薬
Square Dish with Dragon and Cloud Design, Yellow Glaze and Overglaze Red｜
KATO Hajime｜1953｜porcelain, glaze

3 龍 自在置物｜［不詳］｜江戸末〜明治時代｜鉄
Dragon, Articulated Ornament｜[Unknown]｜c. 1860-1912｜iron

1

3

2

1 **変織縮緬訪問着「花」**│木村雨山│昭和40│縮緬、友禅
  Silk Crêpe Kimono: Flower │ KIMURA Uzan │ 1965 │ silk crêpe, yuzen dyed

2 **彫漆木瓜之図筥**│岡田章人│昭和38│木・漆、彫漆
  Box with Japanese Quince Design, Choshitsu Technique │ OKADA Akihito │ 1963 │ wood, lacquer, carved lacquer

3 **乾漆木蓮図硯箱**│二十代 堆朱楊成│大正6│木胎・漆・金・鉛・貝、乾漆・螺鈿
  Inkstone Box with Mulan Magnolia Design, Kanshitsu Technique │ TSUISHU Yozei XX │
  1917 │ wood, lacquer, gold, lead, shell, dry lacquer, raden inlay

1

1 **桃林**｜長谷川良雄｜大正15頃｜紙、水彩、額
Peach Orchard｜HASEGAWA Yoshio｜
c. 1926｜paper, watercolor, framed

2 **白川村**｜黒田重太郎｜明治38｜紙、水彩、額
Shirakawa Village｜KURODA Jutaro｜
1905｜paper, watercolor, framed

2

彼岸 │ 寺島紫明 │
昭和21 │ 絹本、着色、額
Prayer │ TERASHIMA Shimei │
1946 │ color on silk, framed

1

3

2

1 **鰈**｜村上華岳｜大正11｜絹本、着色、軸
 Flatfish｜MURAKAMI Kagaku｜1922｜color on silk, hanging scroll

2 **貝尽くし 牙彫置物**｜安藤緑山｜大正〜昭和初｜象牙、彫刻・着色
 Carved Ivory Figurines of Shellfish｜ANDO Ryokuzan｜c. 1912-30｜ivory, carved, dyed

3 **潮沊**｜西川 實｜昭和42｜陶器・釉薬
 Spring Tide｜NISHIKAWA Minoru｜1967｜ceramic, glaze

1

3

2

1 **桜蝶図平皿**｜並河靖之｜明治時代｜金属・釉薬、有線七宝
   Plate with Cherry Blossoms and Butterflies Design｜NAMIKAWA Yasuyuki｜1868-1912｜metal, glaze, wired cloisonné

2 **香筥 桜花錫椽**｜赤塚自得｜大正時代｜木胎・漆・金・錫、高蒔絵
   Incense Container with Cherry Blossoms Design with Tin Brim｜AKATSUKA Jitoku｜1912-26｜wood, lacquer, gold, tin, taka maki-e

3 **柳桜に垣蒔絵手箱**｜上島光波｜明治時代｜木・漆・金、蒔絵
   Box with Willow and Cherry Blossoms with Hedge Design, Maki-e｜UESHIMA Koha｜1868-1912｜wood, lacquer, gold, maki-e

1

2

1　**春宵**｜黒田 暢｜昭和48｜布、型染、二曲一隻屏風
　Spring Evening｜KURODA Toru｜1973｜cloth, stencil dyed, two-panels folding screen

2　**鈞窯 大鉢**｜木村盛伸｜昭和58｜陶器・釉薬
　Large Bowl, Jun Ware Style｜KIMURA Morinobu｜1983｜ceramic, glaze

1

2

1 **夜桜**｜印藤真楯｜明治30｜画布、油彩、額
   Cherry Blossoms at Night｜INDO Matate｜1897｜oil on canvas, framed

2 **夜桜**｜須田国太郎｜昭和16｜画布、油彩、額
   Cherry Blossoms Reflecting Bonfire｜SUDA Kunitaro｜1941｜oil on canvas, framed

大正時代に描かれた作品ですが、描かれている人々は着物に髷姿。どうやら現実の光景ではなく、江戸時代のころの夜桜を想像で描いたようです。宴会を楽しむ人々や、遠景まで連なる提灯は仔細に描かれているものの、肝心の夜桜は曖昧にしか描かれておらず、不思議な雰囲気につつまれています。村上華岳は、あえかな線の仏画が高く評価された日本画家ですが、本作のような初期の人物描写にも、すでにその片鱗が垣間見えています。

Although drawn in the 1910s, the people depicted are clothed in kimono and wear topknots and traditional chignons. It appears that rather than a scene from reality, this is an imagined scene of evening cherry blossom viewing in the Edo Period. The people enjoying the banquet and the lanterns strung far into the distance are drawn in detail, but the all-important cherry blossoms are only vaguely drawn, giving off an enigmatic atmosphere. Murakami Kagaku was a Japanese-style artist whose proficiency in Buddhist paintings with thin outlines was highly praised. The figures in this early work display glimpses of his technique.

夜桜之図｜村上華岳｜大正2｜絹本、着色、二曲一隻屏風
Evening Scene of Cherry Blossoms Viewing｜MURAKAMI Kagaku｜
1913｜color on silk, two-panels folding screen

1

2

1 **茶店**｜国松桂渓｜明治40｜紙、水彩、額
Teahouse｜KUNIMATSU Keikei｜
1907｜paper, watercolor, framed

2 **嵐山春景**｜伊藤仁三郎｜昭和35-44｜紙、木版
Spring Scene in Arashiyama｜ITO Nisaburo｜
1960-69｜paper, woodblock print

3 **花見図花瓶**｜精巧山
明治～大正時代｜陶器、色絵・金彩（一対）
Flower Vase with Cherry Blossoms Viewing Design｜
Seikosan｜1868-1926｜ceramic, overglaze enamels,
gold paint, pair of flower vases

3

桜｜菊池契月｜昭和4｜
紙本、墨画淡彩、軸
Cherry Blossoms｜
KIKUCHI Keigetsu｜
1929｜sumi ink and tint color on
paper, hanging scroll

晩春

旧暦三月・新暦四月・弥生

《晴明》　新暦四月四日頃
　　　　緑が生き生きと輝き出す

《穀雨》　新暦四月二十日頃
　　　　百穀を潤す雨の恵み

清らかで明るい日差しが降りそそぐ晩春のころ。桜も盛りを迎えます。桜は観て楽しむだけではなく、古くはその年の稲の収穫量を占うものでもありました。花が豊かに長く咲けば豊作に、早く散れば不作に。それゆえ花が散らないように祈る鎮花祭が各地で行われてきました。また京都では、桜が散るとともに疫病が流行ったことから、疫神を鎮める「やすらい祭」が平安のころより続けられています。鬼たちが跳ね踊る中、大きな花傘の下に入ると無病息災を得ることができます。

咲き誇る桜に賑やかさをくわえるように、祇園や上七軒などの花街では舞妓や芸妓による舞踊公演が行われます。甲斐庄楠音の《春宵（花びら）》に描かれているのは、酒に桜の花びらを浸して楽しむ遊女の姿。白塗りの下に刻まれた深い皺や肉厚の腕、淫靡な表情など、本来は美しいはずの遊女をグロテスクに描くことで、美しさの裏に潜む妖しさや欲望を炙り出しているかのようです。

LATE SPRING

3rd Month under Japanese lunisolar calendar | April | *YAYOI*

SEIMEI
[Pure and Clear]

April 4th
Greenery is brightly shining.

KOKUU
[Grain Rains]

April 20th
Blessed rain for all grains.

Clear and bright sunlight shines in the late spring. The cherry blossoms reach their height. From olden times, people enjoyed the blossoms, but they were also used to predict the harvest for that year. If the blossoms bloomed full and long, the harvest would be good; and if the blossoms scattered soon, the harvest would be poor. This is why there are Chinkasai festivals to pray that the flowers will not scatter. In Kyoto, when the blossoms scattered epidemics raged, with Yasurai Festivals to quell epidemics from Heian Period times. As ogres jump and dance, standing under a large flower-umbrella would assure sound health.

As if to add liveliness to the cherries in full bloom, in the Gion and Kamishichiken pleasure quarters dance performances by *maiko* and *geiko* are held. Kainosho Tadaoto's *Spring Night (Petals)* shows a prostitute enjoying dipping flower petals into her sake. Drawing what should be a beautiful prostitute by showing deep wrinkles beneath her thick white makeup, her bulky arms, and her wanton expression, he seems to reveal the grotesqueness and desires that lie beneath beauty.

春宵（花びら）｜甲斐庄楠音
Spring Night (Petals) ｜ KAINOSHO Tadaoto

晩春｜LATE SPRING

1

1 **醍醐之華**｜冨田溪仙｜大正15｜絹本、着色、軸
Cherry Blossoms at Daigo-ji Temple｜TOMITA Keisen｜
1926｜color on silk, hanging scroll

2 **飾筥「醍醐」**｜藤田喬平｜平成7頃｜ガラス
Decorative Box: Daigo｜FUJITA Kyohei｜c. 1995｜glass

3 **春宵（花びら）**｜甲斐庄楠音｜大正10頃｜絹本、着色、額
Spring Night (Petals)｜KAINOSHO Tadaoto｜
c. 1921｜color on silk, framed

4 **花蝶尽し鉢**｜輝山｜
明治～大正時代｜陶器・釉薬、色絵・金彩
Bowl with Plethora of Flowers and Butterflies Design｜Kizan｜
1868-1926｜ceramic, glaze, overglaze enamels, gold paint

5 **花蝶図大鉢**｜七代 錦光山宗兵衛｜明治～大正時代｜
陶器・釉薬、色絵・金彩
Large Bowl with Flowers and Butterflies Design｜
KINKOZAN Sobei VII｜1868-1926｜
ceramic, glaze, overglaze enamels, gold paint

2

3

5

4

1

1　**清水寺図額**｜［不詳］｜明治時代｜絹、刺繍、額
View of Kiyomizu-dera Temple｜［Unknown］｜
1868-1912　｜　silk, embroidery, framed

2　**北野の春**｜霜鳥之彦｜明治39｜紙、水彩、額
Spring in Kitano｜SHIMOTORI Yukihiko｜
1906　｜　paper, watercolor, framed

2

1

2

1 **母仔馬**｜坂本繁二郎｜昭和35｜画布、油彩、額
Horse with Foal｜SAKAMOTO Hanjiro｜
1960｜oil on canvas, framed

2 **粟田口より 四月の夕**｜国枝金三｜［不詳］｜紙、水彩、額
View from Awataguchi: Evening in April｜KUNIEDA Kinzo｜
[n. d.]｜paper, watercolor, framed

鮮魚 ｜ 西村五雲 ｜ 昭和6頃 ｜ 絹本、着色、軸
Fresh Fish ｜ NISHIMURA Goun ｜ c. 1931 ｜ color on silk, hanging scroll

春の夜、霞につつまれて柔らかに光る満月の下に一匹の狐がいます。視線の先には菜の花にとまろうとする黄色い蝶々が。薄い金色の月に、濃い金色の狐、その間には鮮やかな金色の葉がそよいでいます。春のあたたかな夜を寿ぐような、詩情あふれる作品です。作者の竹内栖鳳は京都画壇を代表する作家の一人で、特に動物画の名手として高く評価されました。繊細に描写された対象と、余白の広い悠然とした構図が特徴です。

On a spring night, a fox sits bathed in the soft light of the full moon wrapped in haze. Its gaze is focused on a yellow butterfly about to light on a rapeseed blossom. The light gold colored moon and the dark gold colored fox, and between them flits a bright gold colored butterfly. This work, so full of poetic sentiment, celebrates the warmth of a spring night. The artist, Takeuchi Seiho, was a leading figure of the Kyoto painters group, particularly renowned for his mastery of animal paintings. His characteristic design is that of elegantly drawn subjects contrasted with the calmness of large areas of blank space.

おぼろ月｜竹内栖鳳｜
昭和3｜紙本、着色、軸
Hazy Moon｜TAKEUCHI Seiho｜
1928｜color on paper, hanging scroll

2

1

4

3

1 　二つのアネモネ｜長谷川 潔｜昭和9｜紙、アクアチント
Two Anemones｜HASEGAWA Kiyoshi｜1934｜paper, aquatinte (aquatint)

2 　アネモネ｜長谷川 潔｜昭和5｜紙、ポアント・セーシュ（ドライポイント）
Anemones｜HASEGAWA Kiyoshi｜1930｜paper, pointe sèche (dry point)

3 　鉄描銅彩薊皿｜富本憲吉｜昭和29｜陶器・釉薬
Dish with Thistle Design, Iron and Copper Glaze｜TOMIMOTO Kenkichi｜1954｜ceramic, glaze

4 　七宝あざみ小皿｜藤井達吉｜大正5-12｜銅・釉薬、打ち出し・七宝
Cloisonné Small Dishes With Thistle Design｜FUJII Tatsukichi｜1916-23｜ccopper, glaze, repousse, cloisonné

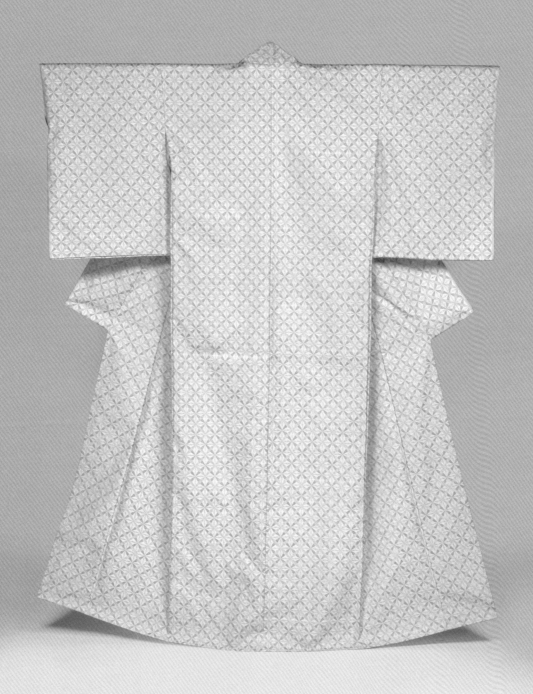

経錦着物「笹の春」｜北村武資｜平成23｜絹、経錦
Kimono of Tate-nishiki Fabric: Bamboo Grass in Spring ｜ KITAMURA Takeshi ｜ 2011 ｜ silk, tate-nishiki weaving

穀雨 ｜ *KOKUU*

2

1 雨中牡丹図｜金田和郎｜大正9頃｜絹本、着色、軸
Peonies in the Rain｜KANADA Waro｜
c. 1920｜color on silk, hanging scroll

2 色絵牡丹蝶之図喰籠｜河村熹太郎｜
昭和初期｜磁器・釉薬、染付・色絵
Covered Box with Butterfly and Peony Design, Overglaze Enamels｜
KAWAMURA Kitaro｜
c. 1926-40｜porcelain, glaze, blue underglaze, overglaze enamels

1

2

1

4

3

1 **音羽焼牡丹唐草花瓶**｜五代 清水六兵衛｜昭和2｜陶器・釉薬
Flower Vase with Peony in Scroll Style, Otowa Ware｜KIYOMIZU Rokubei V｜1927｜ceramic, glaze

2 **瑗白磁牡丹文花瓶**｜三代 清風与平｜明治後期～大正初期｜磁器・釉薬
White Porcelain Flower Vase with Peony Design in Relief｜SEIFU Yohei III｜c. 1895-1920｜porcelain, glaze

3 **豆蒔絵手箱**｜池田泰真｜明治時代｜木・漆・金・鉛・貝、蒔絵・螺鈿
Box with Bean Vine Design｜IKEDA Taishin｜1868-1912｜wood, lacquer, gold, lead, shell, maki-e, raden inlay

4 **蚕豆嫩葉彩画合子**｜河合卯之助｜［不詳］｜陶器・釉薬、色絵
Small Covered Box with Young Broad-bean Leaf, Overglaze Enamels｜KAWAI Unosuke｜[n. d.]｜ceramic, glaze, overglaze enamels

1

前衛表現といえば洋画であった時代に、あえて日本画に
こだわって前衛表現を繰り広げた玉村方久斗。自らホク
ト社を結成して、仲間とともに前衛的な作品を発表し続
けました。またそれだけではなく、当時の生活を窺わせ
る作品も多く残しています。本作は、大輪の芍薬が咲き
誇る庭で、キャッチボールを楽しむ家族の姿を描いたも
の。野球のユニフォームを身につけた子どもや、流行り
の洋装を着た人々が活き活きと描写されています。

In an era when avant-garde expression equaled Western-style
painting, Tamamura Hokuto persisted in formulating avant-
garde expression in Japanese-style paintings. He founded Hokuto
Company and continued to create avant-garde works along with his
circle. He has also left many works which give us observations of
life in his time. This work depicts a family enjoying a game of catch
in a garden where peonies are in full bloom. The boy in the baseball
uniform and the adults in fashionable clothing are drawn with much
vigor.

2

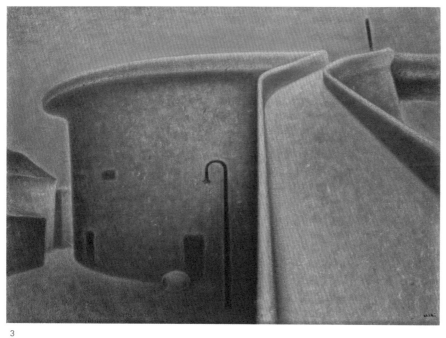

3

1　**休日** | 玉村方久斗 | 昭和6 | 紙本、着色、額
　Holiday | TAMAMURA Hokuto | 1931 | color on paper, framed

2　**Kyoto 24 April 1993** | デイヴィッド・ホックニー | 平成5 | 紙、リトグラフ、額
　Kyoto 24 April 1993 | David HOCKNEY | 1993 | paper, lithograph, framed

3　**晩春** | 牛島憲之 | 昭和29 | 画布、油彩、額
　Late Spring | USHIJIMA Noriyuki | 1954 | oil on canvas, framed

初夏

旧暦四月・新暦五月・卯月

《立夏》　新暦五月五日頃

夏が開く

《小満》　新暦五月二十一日頃

麦が実る

柔らかな光の中、透き通るような空へ向かって若葉が伸び始める初夏の季節。春に顔を出した嵐山の筍も茶色い皮をすっかり脱ぎ捨てるころです。この時季の竹の姿を、福田平八郎の《竹》は大胆な構図で描いています。まださくれ立った筍と、つやつやと成長していく若竹の対比が絶妙な一作です。

五月から六月にかけて、緑に彩りを添えるのが紫の花々。はじめに見ごろを迎えるのは藤で、宇治の平等院では樹齢二百年を超す樹が見事な花棚をつくります。続いて咲くのは、古くから高貴さの象徴とされてきた桐の花。鳳凰が棲む木と言われ、天皇の装束の文様としても使われてきました。この後、梅雨が近づくにつれて、菖蒲、紫陽花と濃淡さまざまな紫の花がひらいていきます。

鮮やかさを増す自然に負けじと行われるのが京都三大祭のひとつ、葵祭。五月十五日には平安時代の衣装に身を包んだ行列がゆったりと進み、市中を雅やかな雰囲気で包みます。

RIKKA
[Beginning of Summer]

May 5th
Summer is starting.

SHOMAN
[Lesser Ripening]

May 21st
Wheat is ripening.

The early summer season, when young leaves start to stretch toward the clear sky in the soft light, is when the bamboo shoots of Arashiyama that peeked out in the spring finish shedding their brown skins. Fukuda Heihachiro's *Bamboo* depicts this season's bamboo in a bold composition. The contrast between the bamboo shoot that still holds its shaggy covering and the smooth, growing young bamboo stalks is masterful.

From May to June purple-hued flowers lend coloration to the greenery. First, wisteria come into blossom on a two-hundred-year-old trunk that blooms on a superb trellis at the Byodoin in Uji. This is followed by pawlonia flowers considered a symbol of nobility from olden times. This tree is said to be where the phoenix dwells, and as such has been chosen for the pattern of the emperor's attire. After this time, as the rainy season nears, irises and hydrangeas in dark and light purple open their flowers.

The Aoi (Hollyhock) Festival, one of Kyoto's three main festivals, takes place in this season as if not to be outdone by the increasing vividness of nature. On May 15, the parade of those attired in costumes of the Heian Period proceed decorously, wrapping the city in an atmosphere of elegance.

竹 | 福田平八郎
Bamboo | FUKUDA Heihachiro
［部分］

初夏 | EARLY SUMMER

1

1 　**浦嶋子図** ｜ 冨田渓仙 ｜ 昭和6 ｜ 絹本、着色、軸（双幅）
　　Urashimako ｜ TOMITA Keisen ｜ 1931 ｜ color on silk, hanging scrolls (diptych)

2 　**葵祭り①** ｜ 伊藤仁三郎 ｜ 昭和35-44 ｜ 紙、木版
　　Aoi Festival 1 ｜ ITO Nisaburo ｜ 1960-69 ｜ paper, woodblock print

3 　**葵祭り②** ｜ 伊藤仁三郎 ｜ 昭和35-44 ｜ 紙、木版
　　Aoi Festival 2 ｜ ITO Nisaburo ｜ 1960-69 ｜ paper, woodblock print

4 　**御所車蒔絵引戸** ｜ 迎田秋悦 ｜ 明治後期～昭和初 ｜ 木・漆、蒔絵、引戸（二面）
　　A Pair of Sliding Doors with Court Carriage Design, Maki-e ｜ KODA Shuetsu ｜ c. 1900-30 ｜ wood, lacquer, maki-e, pair of sliding doors

2

3

4

1

2

1　**藤図花瓶**｜濤川惣助｜明治時代｜金属・釉薬、無線・有線七宝
　Vase with Wisteria Design｜NAMIKAWA Sosuke｜1868-1910｜metal, glaze, non-wired and wired cloisonné

2　**花鳥図香炉**｜錦雲軒稲葉｜明治～大正時代｜金属・釉薬、有線七宝
　Incense Burner with Birds and Flowers Design｜Kin'unken Inaba｜1868-1926｜metal, glaze, wired cloisonné

3　**藤に孔雀図刺繍壁掛**｜［不詳］｜明治38頃｜絹、刺繍
　Tapestry with Peacock and Peahen with Wisteria Design｜[Unknown]｜c.1905｜silk, embroidery

3

息を呑むような総刺繍の壁掛です。枝から一直線に垂れ下がる藤花が、二羽の孔雀の羽根に重なって、絢爛な印象をさらに高めています。地面に咲いているのはタンポポに似た花、ノゲシでしょうか。中央には、同じく初夏に見頃を迎える菖蒲も咲いています。よく見ると、どこかへ飛んで行こうとする一羽の小さな雀が。豪奢な画面の中に混じる一点の素朴な存在に、作者の風流心を感じます。

This tapestry is a breathtaking work covered overall with embroidery. The luxuriant impression is heightened by the straight lines of the wisteria blossoms that hang down overlapping the feathers of the two peacocks. Blooming on the ground are flowers like dandelions, perhaps milk thistles. At the center are irises, which also reach their height of bloom in the early summer. A careful look shows a small sparrow about to fly off. This single simple presence amidst the sumptuous scene is evidence of the artist's refined taste.

1

3

2

1 **竹**｜福田平八郎｜昭和17｜紙本、着色、額
  Bamboo｜FUKUDA Heihachiro｜1942｜color on paper, framed

2 **竹の子に梅 牙彫置物**｜安藤緑山｜大正〜昭和初｜象牙、彫刻・着色
  Carved Ivory Figurine of a Bamboo Shoot with Plums｜ANDO Ryokuzan｜c. 1912-30｜ivory, carved, dyed

3 **花籃「富貴」**｜飯塚琅玕斎｜昭和元頃｜竹
  Flower Basket: Nobleness｜IIZUKA Rokansai｜c. 1926｜bamboo

1

2

1　**罌粟**｜徳岡神泉｜昭和8｜紙本、着色、額
　Poppies｜TOKUOKA Shinsen｜1933｜color on paper, framed

2　**朴の花文庫**｜大下雪香｜昭和10｜木胎・漆・金、蒔絵
　Covered Letter Box with Magnolia Design｜OSHITA Sekko｜1935｜wood, lacquer, gold, maki-e

1 **青華蘭四方花瓶**｜五代 清水六兵衞｜大正13｜磁器・釉薬、染付
  Square Vase with Orchid Design, Blue Underglaze｜KIYOMIZU
  Rokubei V｜1924｜porcelain, glaze, blue underglaze

2 **蓮葉に蛙皿**｜正阿弥勝義｜明治時代｜素銅、平象嵌（金）
  Dish in Shape of Lotus Leaf with Frog｜SHOAMI Katsuyoshi｜
  1868-1912｜copper, inlay (gold)

3 **鯉 自在置物**｜高瀬好山｜明治〜大正時代｜四分一、自在
  Articulated Carp｜TAKASE Kozan｜
  1868-1926｜shibuichi copper alloy, articulated figure

4 **塩釉紅瓷蘭文皿**｜岩淵重哉｜昭和56頃｜陶器・塩釉
  Dish with Orchid Design, Salt Glaze｜IWABUCHI Shigeya｜
  c. 1981｜ceramic, salt glaze

5 **青白磁筆架**｜竹内碧外｜昭和23｜磁器・釉薬、筆架（一対）
  Two Brush Rests, Blueish-White Porcelain｜TAKEUCHI Hekigai｜
  1948｜porcelain, glaze, pair of brush rests

1

2

1　**田植の頃** │ 村上華岳 │ 明治45 │ 紙本、着色、二曲一隻屏風
　Season of Rice Planting │ MURAKAMI Kagaku │ 1912 │ color on paper, two-panels folding screen

2　**三条大橋** │ 近藤浩一路 │ 大正4 │ 紙本、墨画、軸
　Sanjo Bridge │ KONDO Koichiro │ 1925 │ sumi ink on paper, hanging scroll

小満 | *SHOMAN* [Lesser Ripening]

1

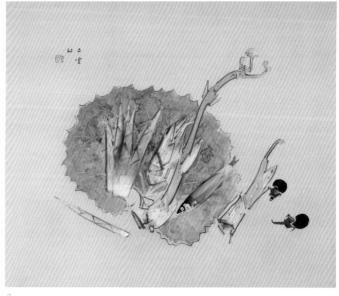

2

1　**雨或いは感傷**｜伊藤久三郎｜
　昭和 12｜画布、油彩、額
　Rainfall or Sentiment｜ITO Kyuzaburo｜
　1937｜oil on canvas, framed

2　**山の幸川の幸**｜西村五雲｜
　昭和 13｜絹本、着色、軸
　Bounty of the Mountains and River｜
　NISHIMURA Goun｜
　1938｜color on silk, hanging scroll

京都の四季を清々しい筆致で描きつづけた宇田荻邨。その写実的な画風は、四条派や大和絵の作品研究に加えて、実際の風景の徹底的なスケッチによって培われました。貴船の光景を描いた本作品は、晩年の傑作のひとつ。群青と緑青のグラデーションによって描かれた豊かな樹々の中で、朱色の神門がひときわ目を惹きます。雨をつかさどる龍神を祀る貴船神社は、京都が豊かな水に恵まれるよう祈りを捧げています。

Uda Tekison depicted Kyoto's four seasons with a fresh touch of his brush. His realistic style was nurtured from his study of the Shijo School and Yamato-e paintings combined with his detailed sketches of actual landscapes. This work of a view of Kibune is one of the masterpieces of his later years. The vermilion shrine gate attracts the viewer's attention among the lush trees drawn in gradations of blues and greens. The dragon god that rules the rain enshrined in Kifune Shrine is worshipped to assure that Kyoto will be blessed with an abundance of water.

水神貴船奥宮 ｜ 宇田荻邨 ｜ 昭和44 ｜ 紙本、着色、額
Inmost Shrine of Kifune Enshrining the God of Water ｜ UDA Tekison ｜ 1969 ｜ color on paper, framed

1 薔薇｜真野紀太郎｜昭和36｜紙、水彩、額
  Roses ｜ MANO Kitaro ｜ 1941 ｜ paper, watercolor, framed

2 薔薇図｜浅井忠｜明治35-40｜紙本、着色、軸
  Roses ｜ ASAI Chu ｜ 1902-07 ｜ color on paper, hanging scroll

3 薔薇と人物｜二代 三木表悦｜昭和7頃｜木・漆
  Rose and Figures ｜ MIKI Hyoetsu II ｜ c. 1932 ｜ wood, lacquer

1

3

2

1 雨後庭園（桂離宮）｜川西 英｜昭和30｜紙、木版
   The Garden after Raining, Katsura Detached Palace｜KAWANISHI Hide｜1955｜paper, woodblock print

2 青瓷大鉢｜清水卯一｜昭和48｜青磁
   Large Celadon Bowl｜SHIMIZU Uichi｜1973｜celadon

3 彫漆延齢草水指｜音丸耕堂｜昭和41｜木胎・漆、彫漆
   Tea Ceremony Water-jar with Japanese Trillium Design｜OTOMARU Kodo｜1966｜wood, lacquer, carved lacquer

1

3

2

1 **麦畑** ｜ 霜鳥之彦 ｜ 明治38 ｜ 紙、水彩、額
  Field of Wheat ｜ SHIMOTORI Yukihiko ｜ 1905 ｜ paper, watercolor, framed

2 **瓢箪に天道虫花瓶** ｜ 正阿弥勝義 ｜ 明治33 ｜ 素銅、象嵌（金・銀・赤銅・緋銅）
  Vase with Gourd and Ladybug Design ｜ SHOAMI Katsuyoshi ｜ 1900 ｜ copper, inlay (gold, silver, akagane, hido)

3 **昆虫文小筥** ｜ 大須賀 喬 ｜ 昭和22 ｜ 洋銀、鍛造・彫金
  Casket with Insects Design ｜ OSUGA Takashi ｜ 1947 ｜ nickel silver, wrought, carved

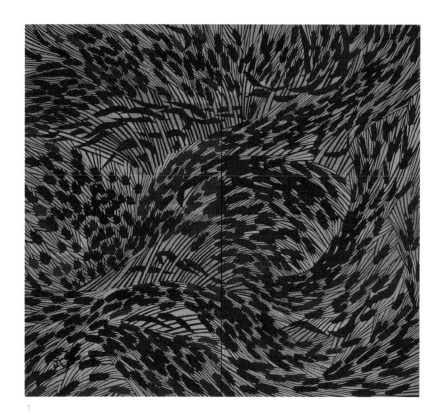

1

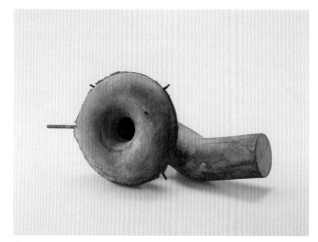

3

2

1　**麦秋** ｜ 西嶋武司 ｜ 昭和38 ｜ 綿、染、二曲一隻屏風
　　Wheat Harvest ｜ NISHIJIMA Takeshi ｜ 1963 ｜ cotton, dyed, two-panels folding screen

2　**かたつむり** ｜ 八木一夫 ｜ 昭和44 ｜ ブロンズ
　　Snail ｜ YAGI Kazuo ｜ 1969 ｜ bronze

3　**揺－75－4** ｜ 森野泰明 ｜ 昭和50 ｜ 陶器・釉薬
　　Vibration-75-4 ｜ MORINO Taimei ｜ 1975 ｜ ceramic, glaze

仲夏

旧暦五月・新暦六月・皐月

《芒種》　新暦六月五日頃

　　　　種を蒔く

《夏至》　新暦六月二十一日頃

　　　　夏に至る

　夏の中ごろ、梅雨の時期。岩倉壽の描く《雨季》のように、どんよりとした雲が空を覆い、雨が降りしきります。鬱陶しい気持ちに捉われがちな季節ですが、一歩外へ出てみると、雨の京都はまた格別の趣。花見小路の石畳を跳ねる雨や、京町屋のひさしから滴る雨粒、光を夜雨に乱反射させながらそびえ立つ京都タワー。実は一番艶やかな季節かもしれません。

　川の水嵩が増すころ、和菓子屋さんの店頭を彩るのが「若鮎」。白い求肥を茶色の焼皮で包んだお菓子で、この時期に鴨川を上ってくる鮎の姿をしています。お店それぞれに独自の形や味があるので、食べ比べをしてみるのも一興です。

　一年の中で最も昼が長い夏至をすぎ、六月末日に行われるのが「夏越の祓」。半年間でたまった穢れを清める儀式で、大きな茅の輪をくぐったり、魔を祓う豆がのった和菓子「水無月」を食したりします。まだ晴れ間は少なく、鴨川沿いのお店が設ける川床で食事をいただく時が待ち遠しい日々です。

MID-SUMMER

5th Month under Japanese lunisolar calendar | June | *SATSUKI*

BOSHU
[Grain Beards and Seeds]

June 5th
Sowing seeds.

GESHI
[Summer Solstice]

June 21st
To the height of summer.

Around mid-summer comes the rainy season, written as "plum rain." As depicted by Iwakura Hisashi in *Rainy Season*, heavy clouds cover the sky and rain falls incessantly. It tends to be a season that feels oppressive, but take a step outdoors and Kyoto in the rain exudes a special elegance. The rain splashing up from the stone pavement of Hanamikoji, the raindrops dripping from the eaves of traditional *machiya* merchant houses, the diffused reflection of light of Kyoto Tower rising up in the night rain. This may actually be Kyoto's most vivid season.

As the water level in the rivers rise, Japanese sweets shops display Young Sweetfish. This sweet is made of white rice cake wrapped in a seared brown covering, presenting the figure of sweetfish that journey up the Kamo River at this time. Each shop offers its own shape and taste, making it a delight to compare the wares.

When the summer solstice's longest daytime in the year passes, "summer purification" rituals are held to cleanse the impurities that have collected over the first half of the year. People pass through a large ring made of sedge reeds or partake of the sweet Minatsuki of triangles of rice jelly topped with adzuki beans said to purify evil spirits. There are still a few clear days, and people long for the time they can dine outside on platforms set out over the Kamo River.

雨季 | 岩倉 壽
Rainy Season | IWAKURA Hisashi

仲夏 | MID-SUMMER

六月の声 (声) | 関根勢之助 | 昭和39 | 画布、油彩、額
Voice of June (Voice) | SEKINE Seinosuke | 1964 | oil on canvas, framed

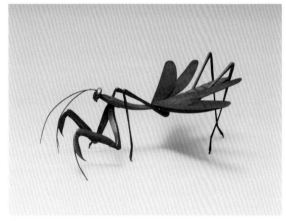

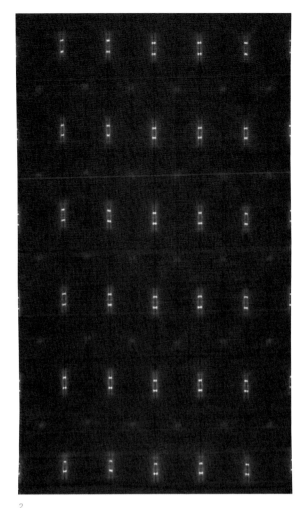

2

1

1 **蟷螂** │ 高瀬好山 │ 大正〜昭和初 │ 鉄、自在
  Mantis │ TAKASE Kozan │ c. 1910-30 │ iron, articulated figure

2 **夏着尺「ともしび」** │ 福本潮子 │ 平成16 │ 夏山絹、藍染・絞染
  Summer Kimono Cloth: Light │ FUKUMOTO Shihoko │ 2004 │ silk, indigo dyed, tie dyed

1929年に東京で生まれ、京都市立美術専門学校（現京都市立芸術大学）で西洋画を学んだ関根勢之助は、油絵、版画、立体など多岐にわたる作品を残しています。中でも1960年代に集中的に制作された油絵作品は、引っ掻いたような細い線と、荒く塗られた色が特徴です。記憶の断片を描き留めたようなその作品は、見る者それぞれの解釈を引き出します。

Born in 1929 in Tokyo, Sekine Seinosuke studied Western-style painting at Kyoto City Technical School of Art (now Kyoto City University of Arts), and has left works in many forms, ranging from oil painting, to woodblock prints, to works in three dimensions. His oil paintings that he worked on in a concentrated way in the 1960s are characterized by thin lines, as if he scratched the surface, and roughly applied colors. These works seem to jot down fragments of memory, inducing viewers to come up with their own interpretations.

1

2

3

1　**紫陽花花瓶**｜六代 清水六兵衞｜昭和16｜陶器・釉薬
　Flower Vase with Hydrangea Design｜KIYOMIZU Rokubei VI｜
　1941｜ceramic, glaze

2　**京鹿の子画瓶**｜河合卯之助｜昭和15｜陶器・釉薬
　Bottle with Japanese Meadowsweet Design｜KAWAI Unosuke｜
　1940｜ceramic, glaze

3　**八仙花**｜平石晃祥｜昭和59｜木・漆
　Hydrangea｜HIRAISHI Kosho｜1984｜wood, lacquer

猫｜林 司馬｜大正末｜絹本、着色、額
Cat｜HAYASHI Shime｜c. 1925｜color on silk, framed

枇杷｜伊藤草白｜
昭和5頃｜紙本、着色、額
Loquats｜ITO Sohaku｜
c. 1930｜color on paper, framed

1

2

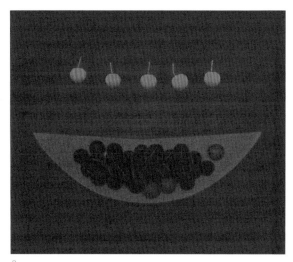

3

1　[題名不詳]｜野島康三｜昭和5｜ブロムオイル・プリント
　　[Title Unknown]｜NOJIMA Yasuzo｜1930｜bromoil print

2　枇杷｜野島康三｜昭和5｜ブロムオイル・プリント
　　Loquats｜NOJIMA Yasuzo｜1930｜bromoil print

3　さくらんぼと青い鉢｜浜口陽三｜昭和51｜紙、メゾチント
　　Cherries and Blue Bowl｜HAMAGUCHI Yozo｜
　　1976｜paper, mezzotint

雨季｜岩倉 壽｜昭和61｜紙本、着色、額
Rainy Season｜IWAKURA Hisashi｜1986｜color on paper, framed

菖蒲 │ 安田靫彦 │ 昭和6 │ 紙本、墨画淡彩、軸
Sweet Flag │ YASUDA Yukihiko │ 1931 │ sumi ink and tint color on paper, hanging scroll

1　**鮎**｜福田平八郎｜昭和25｜絹本、着色、額
Sweetfish｜FUKUDA Heihachiro｜1950｜color on silk, framed

2　**萱草模様螺鈿応用花瓶**｜四代 清水六兵衞｜明治後期｜陶器・釉薬、螺鈿
Vase with Daylily Design, Raden Inlay｜KIYOMIZU Rokubei IV｜c. 1890-1912｜ceramic, glaze, raden inlay

3　**橘文菓子器**｜藤井達吉｜大正5-12｜木、金彩
Sweets Bowl with Tachibana Orange Design｜FUJII Tatsukichi｜1916-23｜wood, gold paint

南禅寺近くの老舗料亭の朝ごはん。まだ夜の暗がりが残るかのように陰を落とした室内に、雅やかな皿を乗せた膳が供されています。半分に割った卵と二尾の海老に魚料理、名物の朝粥はこれから運ばれてくるところでしょうか。近代日本画の三巨匠に数えられる川端龍子は、洋画を学んだのちに日本画に転身した画家です。従来の日本画の繊細な画風を打ち破るような豪胆な大作を多く生み出しました。

Breakfast is set at a long-standing restaurant near Nanzenji Temple. The elegant dishes are placed on the footed tray in a room revealing the remains of shadows from the night's darkness. To accompany the egg split in half and the pair of shrimp and grilled fish, the specialty morning rice porridge may be about to be served. Counted among the three great masters of modern Japanese-style painting, Kawabata Ryushi turned to Japanese-style painting after he had studied Western-style painting. He created many bold masterworks that seemed to overturn the delicacy of Japanese-style painting of the past.

佳人好在｜川端龍子｜大正14｜絹本、着色、額
Summer Parlor｜KAWABATA Ryushi｜1925｜color on silk, framed

1　**動物園**｜須田国太郎｜昭和28｜画布、油彩、額
Zoo｜SUDA Kunitaro｜1953｜oil on canvas, framed

2　**糺の祠**｜加藤源之助｜明治40｜紙、水彩、額
Small Shrine in Tadasu-no-mori Forest｜KATO Gen'nosuke｜1907｜paper, watercolor, framed

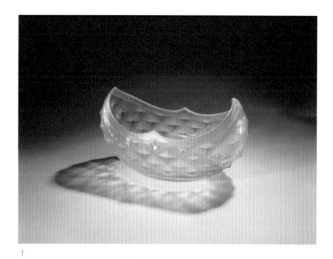

1

2

1　**クリスタル花器**｜佐藤潤四郎｜昭和22｜クリスタルガラス
　　Crystal Flower Vase｜SATO Junshiro｜
　　1947｜crystal glass

2　**硝子鉢**｜各務鑛三｜昭和15｜クリスタルガラス
　　Glass Bowl｜KAGAMI Kozo｜1940｜crystal glass

3　**天藍釉壺「流」**｜叶 光夫｜昭和39｜磁器・釉薬
　　Vase with Indigo Cobalt Glaze: Flowing｜KANO Mitsuo｜
　　1964｜porcelain, glaze

3

下鴨神社夏越神事 ｜ 千種掃雲 ｜［不詳］｜ 絹本、着色、軸
Summer Shinto Ritual at Shimogamo-jinja Shrine ｜
CHIGUSA Soun ｜ [n. d.] ｜ color on silk, hanging scroll

木版摺更紗着物「芹花文」｜鈴田照次｜昭和52｜絹紬、木版
Woodblock Dyed Calico Kimono: Pattern of Japanese Parsely Flower ｜ SUZUTA Teruji ｜ 1977 ｜ silk pongee, woodblock dyed

晩夏

旧暦六月・新暦七月・水無月

《小暑》

新暦七月七日頃

蓮の花が開く

《大暑》

新暦七月二十二日頃

梅雨が明ける

梅雨が明け、煮えつくような暑さがやってくる晩夏。こんな時は、涼しい朝だけにひらく極楽浄土に出かけましょう。相国寺や三室戸寺、法金剛院の境内の池には、とりどりの蓮が一面に咲き、この世ならぬ光景が現出します。あえて日中の暑さを楽しむのも良し。池田洛中の《公園夏日》には、炎天下の円山公園で遊ぶ人々が描かれています。むせかえるような濃密な緑に、人々のモダンな服が爽やかに映えます。

コンコンチキチン、コンチキチン——七月に入ってこの特徴的な囃子の音が四条界隈に響き出すと、祇園祭の幕開けです。平安時代から疫病退散を祈るために行われている八坂神社の祭礼で、一ヶ月にわたってさまざまな神事が執り行われます。一番の見所は、美しく飾られた二十三基の山鉾を曳く山鉾巡業。たくさんの人を乗せた重い山鉾を方向転換させるたびに、沿道から歓声が湧きます。夏の終わりといえど、京都の熱はまだまだ冷めそうにありません。

LATE SUMMER

6th Month under Japanese lunisolar calendar | July | MINAZUKI

SHOSHO
[Lesser Heat]

July 7th
Lotus is blooming.

TAISHO
[Greater Heat]

July 22nd
Rainy Season is over.

As the rainy season ends, late summer brings its broiling heat. On those days, let us go out to see the flowers of paradise which bloom only in the cool mornings. Varieties of lotuses bloom in the ponds of the temples of Shokoku-ji, Mimuroto-ji, and Hokongo-in, offering an otherworldly scene. Or it is possible to enjoy the heat of the mid-day. Ikeda Rakuchu's *Summer Afternoon at a Park* shows people playing under the bright sun in Maruyama Park. The modern clothing of the people contrasts vividly with the suffocating, dense greenery.

"Kon-kon-chiki-chin, kon-chiki-chin"—this unique musical refrain begins to echo in the Shijo area in July, signaling the start of the Gion Festival. This is a month-long variety of Shinto rituals of the Yasaka Shrine to pray for protection from the plague held since the Heian Period. The highlight is the procession of twenty-three gorgeously decorated floats. In order to turn the floats which are full of people, shouts of encouragement rise from those along the route. Summer may be ending, but Kyoto's fever shows no signs of cooling.

公園夏日 | 池田洛中
Summer Afternoon at a Park | IKEDA Rakuchu

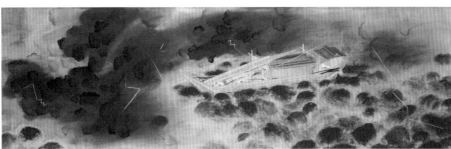

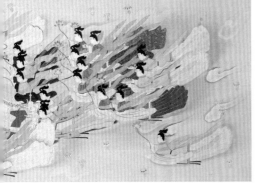
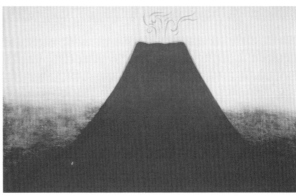

2

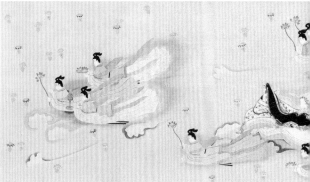

1

1 **竹取物語**｜小林古径｜大正6｜紙本、着色、巻子
   The Tale of the Bamboo Cutter｜KOBAYASHI Kokei｜1917｜color on paper, hand scroll

2 **七夕様（竹取物語より）**｜松原直子｜昭和40｜紙、木版
   Star Festival from "The Tale of the Bamboo Cutter"｜MATSUBARA Naoko｜1965｜paper, woodblock print

北沢映月は、上村松園や土田麦僊らに学んだ女性の日本画家です。歴史上や日常の女性を凛とした姿で描いた作品が多く、繊細な描線にはっきりとした色彩、際立つ装飾模様の描写が特徴です。本作は祇園会（祇園祭）の時期に室内でくつろぐ母娘を描いたもの。左の女の子は小さな山鉾のおもちゃで遊んでいます。江戸時代中期より山鉾は女人禁制とされ、現在でも女性が巡行に参加することはほとんど適いません。

Kitazawa Eigetsu is a female Japanese-style painter who studied under Uemura Shoen and Tsuchida Bakusen. In many of her works she has drawn historical or everyday women in a dignified manner. Characteristic of her depictions are vivid hues within a delicate outline and striking decorative patterns. This painting is of a mother and her daughters relaxing indoors during the period of the Gion Festival. The girl on the left plays with a toy float. From the mid-Edo Period, women have been banned from riding on the floats; even now women hardly ever participate in the procession of the Gion Festival floats.

祇園会｜北沢映月｜昭和11｜絹本、着色、二曲一隻屏風
Gion Festival｜KITAZAWA Eigetsu｜1936｜color on silk, two-panels folding screen

1

2

1 **布象嵌「末摘花」**｜三浦景生｜昭和47｜麻、染・布象嵌、二曲一隻屏風
  Cloth Inlay: Suetsumuhana (Safflower)｜MIURA Kageo｜1972｜hemp, dyed, cloth inlay, two-panels folding screen

2 **胡瓜 牙彫置物**｜安藤緑山｜大正～昭和初｜象牙、彫刻・着色
  Carved Ivory Figurine of Cucumber｜ANDO Ryokuzan｜c. 1912-30｜ivory, carved, dyed

1

2

1　**白蓮図**│榊原紫峰│昭和3頃│絹本、着色、軸
White Lotus│SAKAKIBARA Shiho│c. 1928│color on silk, hanging scroll

2　**睡蓮置物**│六代 清水六兵衞│昭和9│陶器・釉薬
Water Lily Ornament│KIYOMIZU Rokubei VI│1934│ceramic, glaze

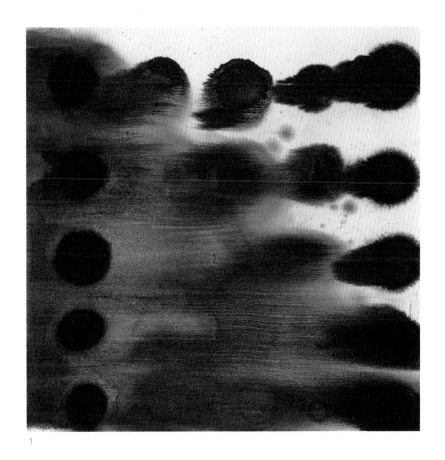

1

2

1 **蓮池**｜堂本尚郎｜平成17｜画布、油彩、額
  Lotus Pond｜DOMOTO Hisao｜2005｜oil on canvas, framed

2 **水蓮の池**｜ケヴィン・マルティーニ＝フュラー｜昭和57｜ゼラチン・シルバー・プリント
  Lilly Pond｜Kevin MARTINI-FULLER｜1982｜gelatin silver print

夕立 ｜ 不動立山 ｜ 昭和5 ｜ 絹本、着色、額
Shower ｜ FUDO Ritsuzan ｜ 1930 ｜ color on silk, framed

1

2

3

1 **仙人掌文香盆**｜大須賀 喬｜昭和11｜赤銅、鍛造・彫金
Incense Tray with Cactus Design｜OSUGA Takashi｜
1936｜red copper, wrought, carved

2 **色絵銀彩合歓双雀図筥**｜藤本能道｜
昭和57｜磁器・釉薬、色絵、銀彩
Box with a Pair of Sparrows and Silk Tree Leaves Design, Overglaze
Enamels and Silver｜FUJIMOTO Yoshimichi｜1982｜
porcelain, glaze, overglaze enamels, silver paint

3 **黄楊浄香座**｜竹内碧外｜昭和25｜黄楊木・陶器
Incense Stand with Lotus Design, Boxwood｜TAKEUCHI Hekigai｜
1950｜boxwood, ceramic

日本の夏 │ ハンナ・ヘーヒ │ 昭和41 │ 紙、コラージュ、額
Summer in Japan │ Hannah HÖCH │ 1966 │ paper, collage, framed

八朔 ｜ 三輪良平 ｜ 平成15 ｜ 紙本、着色、額
Gion's Hassaku (The First Day of the Eighth Month of the Ancent Japanese Calendar) ｜ MIWA Ryohei ｜ 2003 ｜ color on paper, framed

尾鰭をひらひらと翻して泳ぐ姿が涼やかなことから、夏の風物詩として馴染み深い金魚。仏教では八吉祥のひとつとして、運気の向上や精神的な解放をあらわします。八木一艸は、陶芸を絵画や彫刻とならぶ芸術表現だと考え、やきものの技術を使って彫刻的な造形表現を試みた作家です。ところどころ赤味を帯びた釉薬のグラデーションがなんとも美しい一作です。

Goldfish are familiar evocations of summer as the way they swim, tails waving back and forth, gives off a cooling air. In Buddhism they are counted among the eight auspicious omens and embody improving fortune and spiritual liberation. Yagi Isso considered ceramics as an artistic expression on par with painting and sculpture, and sought to create sculptural design elements with ceramic techniques. The gradation in the glaze that here and there appears reddish brings out the beauty in this work.

均窯金魚置物 ｜ 八木一艸 ｜ 昭和35頃 ｜ 陶器・釉薬
Goldfish Ornament in Jun Ware Style ｜ YAGI Isso ｜ c. 1960 ｜ ceramic, glaze

1

3

2

1　**金魚**｜丸岡比呂史｜大正末｜絹本、着色、軸
　　Goldfish｜MARUOKA Hiroshi｜c. 1925｜color on silk, hanging scroll

2　**金魚屋**｜浅野竹二｜昭和28｜紙、木版
　　Goldfish Vendor｜ASANO Takeji｜1953｜paper, woodblock print

3　**金魚**｜北村今三｜昭和7頃｜紙、木版・着色
　　Goldfish｜KITAMURA Imazo｜c. 1932｜paper, woodblock print, hand colored

1

3

2

1　公園夏日｜池田洛中｜昭和8｜絹本、着色、額
Summer Afternoon at a Park ｜ IKEDA Rakuchu ｜
1933 ｜ color on silk, framed

2　洛北の農家｜太田喜二郎｜
大正13｜画布、油彩、額
A Farmhouse of Rakuhoku (Northern Area of Kyoto) ｜
OTA Kijiro ｜ 1924 ｜ oil on canvas, framed

3　兜虫｜高瀬好山｜大正〜昭和初｜鉄、自在
Beetle ｜ TAKASE Kozan ｜
c. 1912-30 ｜ iron, articulated figure

1

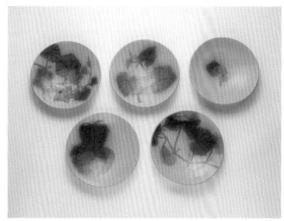

1

1

1　**夏座敷**｜磯田又一郎｜昭和11｜紙本、着色、二曲一隻屏風
Summer Interior Scene｜ISODA Mataichiro｜
1936｜color on paper, two-panels folding screen

2　**京かぼちゃ組皿**｜徳力牧之助｜昭和50｜陶器・釉薬
Dishes with Shishigadani Pumpkin Design｜
TOKURIKI Makinosuke｜1975｜ceramic, glaze

3　**氷屋（於大極殿前）**｜霜鳥之彦｜明治37｜紙、水彩、額
Summer Teahouse in Front of Taikyokuden｜
SHIMOTORI Yukihiko｜1904｜paper, watercolor, framed

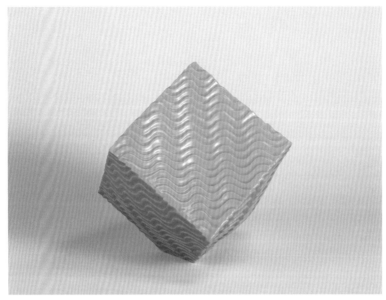

1

2

1　**海**｜三代 宮永東山（宮永理吉）｜昭和48｜磁器・釉薬
　Ocean｜MIYANAGA Tozan III (MIYANAGA Rikichi)｜1973｜porcelain, glaze

2　**水貝蒔絵内朱七寸重箱**｜富田幸七｜明治時代｜木・漆・金、蒔絵
　Tiered Boxes with Shells Design, Maki-e｜TOMITA Koshichi｜1868-1912｜wood, lacquer, gold, maki-e

紅型上布竹文夏長着 ｜ 鎌倉芳太郎 ｜ 昭和43 ｜ 芭蕉布、紅型染
Summer Kimono with Bamboo Design ｜ KAMAKURA Yoshitaro ｜ 1968 ｜ banana-leaf cloth, Bingata stencil dyed

初秋

旧暦七月・新暦八月・文月

《立秋》　　新暦八月七日頃

深い霧が立つ

《処暑》　　新暦八月二十三日頃

稲が実る

うだるような炎暑がつづきますが、暦の上では「立秋」。秋が始まります。耳をすませば、油蝉よりもつくつく法師の声が大きくなっているのに気がつくでしょう。夏のあいだに穫れた瓜やトウモロコシ、大輪の花をひらく向日葵ともそろそろお別れです。黒田辰秋は熟れた瓜のころんとした形を模して、抹茶を入れる茶器を仕立てました。艶めく黒漆につけられた螺鈿の縞が虹色に輝いて、眩惑的な魅力を放ちます。

八月の京都でもっとも重要な行事といえば、なんといっても「五山の送り火」。お盆に迎えた先祖の霊を彼岸へとお送りする精霊送りの行事です。十六日の夜八時、京都の街を囲むようにそびえる五つの山に、「大文字」「妙法」「船形」「左大文字」「鳥居形」の火が次々と点っていきます。人々は、あかあかとした火を見つめながらしずかに祈りを捧げます。火が燃え尽きた後にやってくる寂しさとともに、秋の気配も忍び寄るようです。

EARLY AUTUMN

7th Month under Japanese lunisolar calendar | August | *FUMIZUKI*

RISSHU
[Beginning of Autumn]

August 7th
Thick fog is forming.

SHOSHO
[Manageable Heat]

August 23rd
Rice plant is ripening.

Though the broiling, languid heat continues, according to the almanac it is the Beginning of Autumn (Risshu). Autumn has begun. If you strain your ears you can notice that the sound of the autumn cicada is louder than that of the large brown cicada of high summer. It is time to bid farewell to the melons and corn harvested during the summer, and also to the sunflowers with their large blooms. Kuroda Tatsuaki took the rounded shape of a ripe melon to fashion a tea caddy for powdered matcha tea. The mother-of-pearl inlay stripes placed on the sheen of the black lacquer gleams in rainbow colors, giving off a dazzling allure.

The most important event in August in Kyoto is no doubt the ceremonial bonfires on five mountains. This is a rite to send off the spirits of departed ancestors who were welcomed back during the Obon season. At eight o'clock on the night of the 16th, bonfires are lit consecutively on five mountains surrounding the city, starting with the large Daimonji, then Myoho, then Funagata (boat shape), the Left Daimonji, and finally the Toriigata (shrine gate shape). People quietly offer their prayers as they gaze at the red flames. Along with the sense of loneliness that settles in after the flames are extinguished, it seems a hint of autumn creeps into the days.

螺鈿瓜形棗｜黒田辰秋
Raden Inlayed Melon-shaped Tea Caddy｜KURODA Tatsuaki

初秋｜EARLY AUTUMN

着物「七夕」｜志村ふくみ｜昭和35｜絹・茜・蘇芳・刈安・藍、紬織
Kimono: Star Festival｜SHIMURA Fukumi｜1960｜silk, madder, sappanwood, kariyasu (miscanthus tinctorius), indigo, pongee waeving

七夕｜林 司馬｜昭和13｜絹本、着色、額
Star Festival｜HAYASHI Shime｜1938｜color on silk, framed

2

1

3

1 **無題—1（ひまわりの花）**｜伊島 薫｜昭和64｜ポラロイド（20×24）
  Untitled-1 (Sunflower)｜IJIMA Kaoru｜1989｜polaloid (20×24)

2 **向日葵**｜ポール・カポニグロ｜昭和40｜ゼラチン・シルバー・プリント
  Sunflower｜Paul CAPONIGRO｜1965｜gelatin silver print

3 **三彩向日葵飾皿**｜六代 清水六兵衞｜昭和29｜陶器・釉薬
  Ornamental Dish with Sun Flowers Design, Tri-colored Enameled Glaze｜KIYOMIZU Rokubei VI｜1954｜ceramic, glaze

4 **桃**｜安井曾太郎｜昭和25｜画布、油彩、額
  Peaches｜YASUI Sotaro｜1950｜oil on canvas, framed

4

フランスに留学し、ルノワールやセザンヌらに強い影響を受けた安井曾太郎は、帰国後、日本の風物を油絵でいかに表現するかを模索しました。たどり着いたのは、鮮やかな色彩と躍動感溢れる筆致、緊張感のある構成方法。初秋に収穫期を迎える桃を描いた本作は、あえて歪んだように描かれた机と、その端に置かれた桃が絶妙なバランスを構成しています。緑や黄、赤色の桃のみを丁寧に塗り込むことで、その存在感を強めています。

Studying abroad in France where he was strongly influenced by Renoir and Cezanne, upon his return to Japan, Yasui Sotaro pursued ways to express Japanese scenes in oils. He alighted on brushwork using a bright color palette and lively movement and a tension-filled composition. In this work depicting peaches that are harvested in early autumn, the composition attains a subtle balance between the intentionally warped drawing of the table and the peaches set on the table's edge. By filling in with care only the peaches with green, yellow, and red colors, their presence is enhanced.

1

2

1 **閑日**｜西村五雲｜昭和6｜絹本、着色、軸
After Noon｜NISHIMURA Goun｜1931｜color on silk, hanging scroll

2 **名家畫帖「画苑」より**｜鈴木松年｜明治後期｜絹本、着色、画帖
from Booklet with Famous Artists "Picture Garden"｜SUZUKI Shonen｜c. 1890-1912｜color on silk, booklet

1

4

2

3

1 　**葛に蜘蛛の巣図文庫**｜旭 玉山｜明治43｜木・鉛・貝、螺鈿
Letter Box with Kudzu Vine and Spider Web Design｜
ASAHI Gyokuzan｜1910｜wood, lead, shell, raden inlay

2 　**螺鈿瓜形棗**｜黒田辰秋｜昭和24｜木・漆・貝、螺鈿
Raden Inlayed Melon-shaped Tea Caddy｜KURODA Tatsuaki｜
1949｜wood, lacquer, shell, raden inlay

3 　**瓜形香炉**｜川原林秀国｜明治23｜銀、平象嵌（金・素銅）
Oriental-Melon-shaped Incense Burner｜
KAWARABAYASHI Hidekuni｜1890｜silver, inlay (gold, copper)

4 　**玉蜀黍 牙彫置物**｜安藤緑山｜大正〜昭和初｜象牙、彫刻・着色
Carved Ivory Figurine of Corn｜ANDO Ryokuzan｜
c. 1912-30｜ivory, carved, dyed

3

1

2

1　色鍋島笹輪文鉢｜十三代 今泉今右衛門｜昭和42｜磁器・釉薬
　　Dish with Circled Bamboo-grass Design, Overglaze Enameled Nabeshima Ware｜IMAIZUMI Imaemon XIII｜1967｜porcelain, glaze

2　鉄薬丸紋鉢（丸紋笹絵鉢）｜河井寬次郎｜昭和16｜陶器・釉薬、轆轤成形
　　Iron Glazed Bowl with Circle Pattern Design｜KAWAI Kanjiro｜1941｜ceramic, glaze, wheel making

3　秋立つ｜二代 田辺竹雲斎｜昭和60｜竹
　　Beginning of Autumn｜TANABE Chiku'unsai II｜1985｜bamboo

1

2

1 **初秋** | 野島康三 | 昭和5 | ブロムオイル・プリント
  Early Autumn | NOJIMA Yasuzo | 1930 | bromoil print

2 **庭の隅所見** | 野島康三 | 昭和5 | ブロムオイル・プリント
  A View of the Garden Corner | NOJIMA Yasuzo | 1930 | bromoil prin

2

1

3

1 **朝顔**｜土田麦僊｜昭和3｜紙本、着色、二曲一双屏風
Morning Glories｜TSUCHIDA Bakusen｜
1928｜color on paper, pair of two-panels folding screens

2 **朝顔の図彫宝石筥**｜音丸耕堂｜昭和15｜木・漆、彫漆
Carved Jewelry Box with Morning Glories Design｜
OTOMARU Kodo｜1940｜wood, lacquer, carved lacquer

3 **朝顔等**｜吉原治良｜昭和3｜画布、油彩、額
Morning Glories and Marine Products｜
YOSHIHARA Jiro｜1928｜oil on canvas, framed

清晨｜福田平八郎｜昭和10｜絹本、着色、軸
Cool Morning｜FUKUDA Heihachiro｜
1935｜color on silk, hanging scroll

2

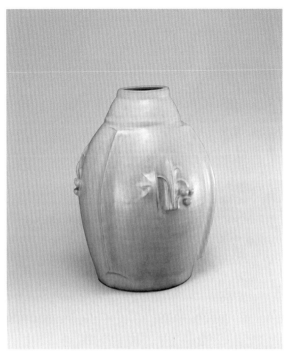

1

3

1 　**清晨** ｜ 深見陶治 ｜ 昭和 59 ｜ 磁器・釉薬
　　Cool Morning ｜ FUKAMI Toji ｜ 1984 ｜ porcelain, glaze

2 　**葡萄文花瓶** ｜ 楠部彌弌 ｜ 昭和 2 ｜ 陶器・釉薬
　　Flower Vase with Grapevine Design ｜ KUSUBE Yaichi ｜ 1927 ｜ ceramic, glaze

3 　**楽焼葡萄文花入** ｜ バーナード・リーチ ｜ ［不詳］ ｜ 陶器・釉薬
　　Vase with Grape and Vine Leaf Design, Raku Ware ｜ Bernard LEACH ｜ [n. d.] ｜ ceramic, glaze

1

2

1　**秋茄子と黒茶碗**｜速水御舟｜大正10｜絹本、着色、額
 Autumn Eggplants and Black Teabowl｜HAYAMI Gyoshu｜1921｜color on silk, framed

2　**柘榴に蝉飾器**｜正阿弥勝義｜明治時代｜銅、象嵌（金・赤銅・四分一）
 Covered Jar in Shape of Pomegranate and Cicada｜SHOAMI Katsuyoshi｜1868-1912｜copper , inlay (gold, akagane, shibuichi copper alloy)

秋の空気が満ちてくるころに姿をあらわす赤とんぼ。その形や色の麗しさから、秋の景物として古くから工芸品につけられてきました。また、前へ前へと一直線に進む姿が勝利を連想させるとして、武具の文様ともなってきました。松田権六は、加賀蒔絵の伝統に根ざしながら、新しい漆表現の立脚に貢献した漆芸家です。本作では、たおやかに叢生するすすきの中を群れ飛ぶ赤とんぼの姿が、格調高く表現されています。

Red dragonflies appear as the autumn air permeates the season. For the delicacy of their shape and coloring, dragonflies have adorned craftworks from ancient times as a natural feature of autumn. The way dragonflies advance straight ahead has been associated with victory, and used as a design on arms and armor. While steeped in the tradition of Kaga makie lacquerware, lacquer artist Matsuda Gonroku contributed to defining a new expression for lacquerware. This work is a lofty representation of a swarm of dragonflies flying among the dense growth of graceful silver grass.

蒔絵箱「赤とんぼ」｜松田権六｜昭和44｜木胎・金・貝、蒔絵・螺鈿
Casket with Red Dragonflies Design, Maki-e｜MATSUDA Gonroku｜1969｜wood, gold, mother-of-pearl, maki-e, raden inlay

むくげと野草模様着物 ｜ 稲垣稔次郎 ｜ 昭和35 ｜ 絹、型絵染
Kimono with Roses of Sharon and Wildflowers Design ｜ INAGAKI Toshijiro ｜ 1960 ｜ silk, stencil dyed

1

2

1　**舞妓**｜小倉遊亀｜昭和44｜紙本、着色、額
Maiko Maiden｜OGURA Yuki｜1969｜color on paper, framed

2　**色絵飾筥**｜富本憲吉｜昭和16｜磁器・釉薬、色絵
Ornamental Hexagonal Box, Overglaze Enamels｜TOMIMOTO Kenkichi｜1970｜porcelain, glaze, overglaze enamels

仲秋　旧暦八月・新暦九月・葉月

《白露》　新暦九月七日頃
　　　　　白い露が宿る

《秋分》　新暦九月二十二日頃
　　　　　虫が冬支度を始める

月がひときわ煌々と輝く九月の中ごろ。仲秋の名月と呼ばれるこの月を、平安時代の貴族たちは池や酒杯に映したり、詩歌を詠じたりして楽しみました。こうした心は今でも変わらず、京都の各所で、舟を浮かべたり、お茶や音楽とともに月を愛でる会がひらかれています。

秋分の日を中日として、その前後七日間は秋のお彼岸。「暑さ寒さも彼岸まで」と言う通り、このころを境に京都もすっかり涼やかになります。街のあちらこちらで萩、女郎花、葛、藤袴、薄、撫子、桔梗の七草が咲き溢れ、その落ち着いた色合いに秋をしみじみと感じます。草花だけではなく、稲や栗などもたわわに実るころ。神社では五穀豊穣に感謝する神事が執り行われ、和菓子屋さんには栗きんとんや栗かのこなど、味わい豊かな秋の味覚がならびます。銅版画の大家、長谷川潔の《くりとかたつむり》では、銅版画特有の濃やかな線を生かして、栗のイガや鬼皮が見事に表現されています。

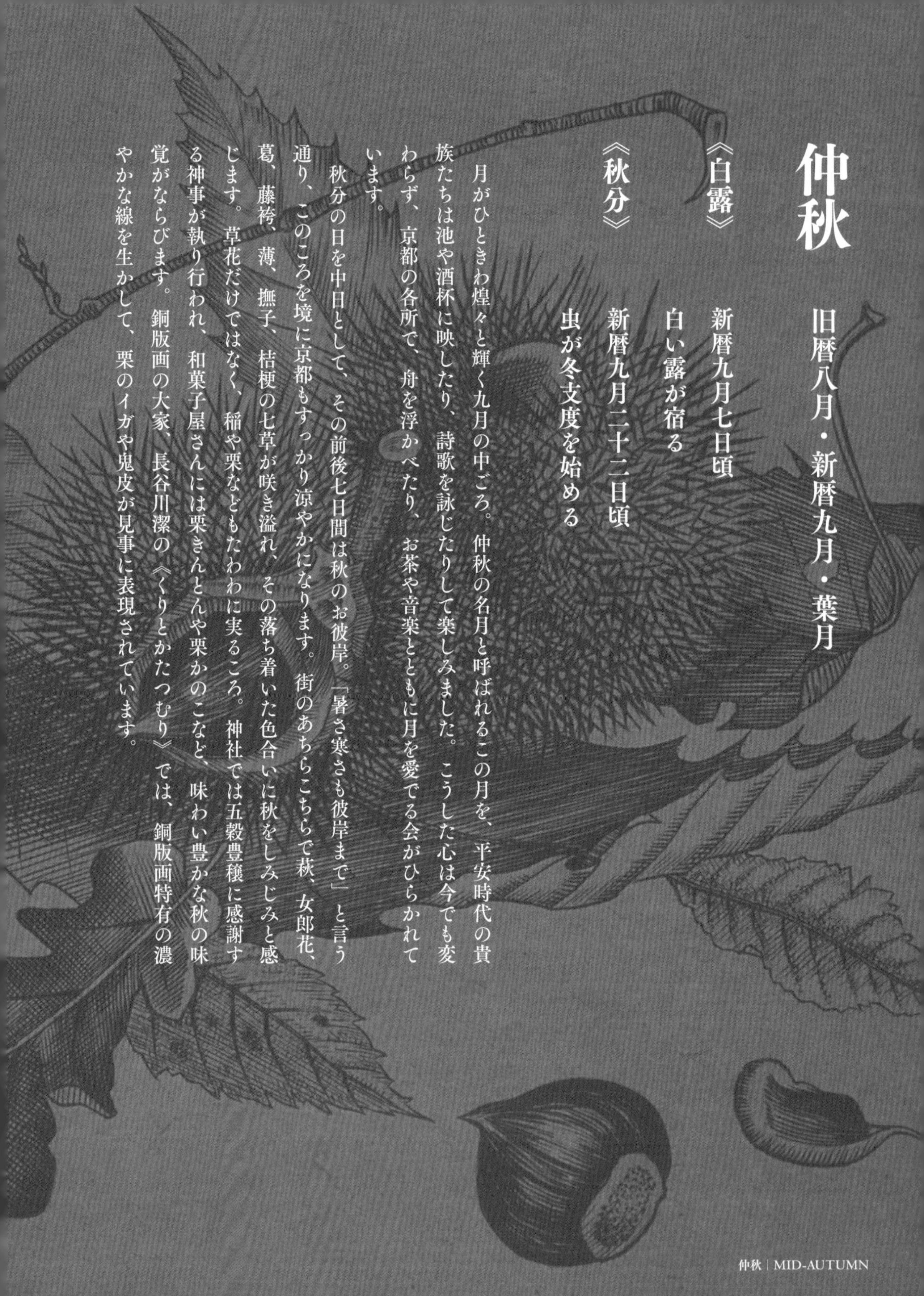

MID-AUTUMN

8th Month under Japanese lunisolar calendar || September || *HAZUKI*

HAKURO
[White Dew]

September 7th
White dew is falling.

SHUBUN
[Autumn Equinox]

September 22nd
Insects are preparing for the coming winter.

Mid-September is when the moon shines with a special brilliance. The Heian Period courtiers took pleasure in this mid-autumn harvest moon's reflection on a pond or in a sake cup, and through writing and reciting poems. These sentiments have not changed, as seen in many places in Kyoto where gatherings are held on boats, and moon viewings are accompanied by tea or music.

The seven-day period surrounding the autumn equinox is a time to observe Buddhist rituals. As the saying goes, "the heat and the cold last until the equinox," and Kyoto starts to cool down after this time. The seven autumnal plants—bush clover, silvergrass, kudzu, fringed pink, golden lace, thoroughwort, balloon flower—bloom throughout the city, their subdued colors infused with the pathos of fall. This is also the time when rice and chestnuts fully ripen. Shrines hold rites in gratitude for abundant crops, and Japanese sweets shops display tasty autumn chestnut sweets. In *Chestnuts and a Snail*, Hasegawa Kiyoshi, the masterful etcher, brings out the deep lines particular to etchings in a superb representation of the bur and shell of the chestnut.

くりとかたつむり｜長谷川 潔
Chestnuts and a Snail｜HASEGAWA Kiyoshi

仲秋｜MID-AUTUMN

白露 | *HAKURO* [White Dew]

美しく着飾った女性と子どもが秋の空に立った虹を見上げています。座る女性の背後に咲いているのは、秋の七草のひとつである萩。夏の虹はくっきりと大輪を描くのに対して、秋の虹は色が淡く、すぐに消えてゆくことから、はかなさをあらわす風物とされてきました。上村松園は美人画の名手として知られ、女性で初めて文化勲章を受章した日本画家です。唇や指先などの細部まで、しとやかさと凛々しさが漲る描写がなされています。

Beautifully attired women and a child look up at a rainbow spanning the autumn sky. Blooming at the back of the seated woman is bush clover, one of the seven autumnal grasses. In contrast to summer rainbows that form a clear, large arc, autumn rainbows are faintly colored, and they disappear quickly. This has made them a natural feature that expresses the ephemeral quality of the seasons. The first woman to have been awarded Japan's Order of Cultural Merit, Japanese-style painter Uemura Shoen is known for her skill in depicting beautiful women. The dignified nature of the women pervades the painting in every detail from their lips to the tips of their fingers.

虹を見る｜上村松園｜昭和7｜絹本、着色、二曲一双屏風
Looking up at the Rainbow｜UEMURA Shoen｜1932｜color on silk, pair of two-panels folding screens

菊花節｜鏑木清方｜昭和17｜絹本、着色、軸
The Chrysanthemum Festival｜
KABURAKI Kiyokata｜
1942｜color on silk, hanging scroll

1

2

1 **萩と茶屋** │ 田中善之助 │ 明治40頃 │ 紙、水彩、額
  Bush Clover and a Teahouse │ TANAKA Zen'nosuke │ c. 1907 │ paper, watercolor, framed

2 **色絵秋草手焙** │ 五代 清水六兵衞 │ 昭和15 │ 陶器・釉薬、色絵
  Covered Brazier with Autumn Wild Flowers Design, Overglaze Enamels │ KIYOMIZU Rokubei V │ 1940 │ ceramic, glaze, overglaze enamels

1

3

2

4

1 **妖炎** │ 春日井路子 │ 平成5 │ 布、染、二曲一隻屏風
Mysterious Flame │ KASUGAI Michiko │ 1993 │ cloth, dyed, two-panels folding screen

2 **焰** │ 岩田久利 │ 昭和55 │ ガラス
Flames │ IWATA Hisatoshi │ 1980 │ glass

3 **鶏頭文乱箱** │ 藤井達吉 │ ［不詳］ │ 木・鉛、象嵌・着色
Clothes Tray with Cockscomb Design │ FUJII Tatsukichi │ [n. d.] │ wood, lead, inlay, hand colored

4 **白露** │ 山口華楊 │ 昭和49 │ 紙本、着色、額
White Dew (Early Autumn) │ YAMAGUCHI Kayo │ 1974 │ color on paper, framed

1

2

1　**南瓜なとの静物**｜伊谷賢蔵｜昭和34｜画布、油彩、額
　Pumpkin and Other Still Life｜ITANI Kenzo｜1959｜oil on canvas, framed

2　**銀象嵌鉄鴫文箱**｜増田三男｜昭和42｜鉄・銀、鍛造・象嵌
　Box with Snipes Design, Silver Inlay｜MASUDA Mitsuo｜1967｜iron, silver, wrought, inlay

3　**朧夜**｜池田遥邨｜昭和57｜紙本、着色、額
　Dim Moonlight｜IKEDA Yoson｜1982｜color on paper, framed

白露 | *HAKURO*

1

3   2

秋分｜*SHUBUN* [Autumn Equinox]

---

1 **秋風**｜結城素明｜昭和初期｜絹本、着色、軸
   Autumn Breeze｜YUKI Somei｜c. 1926-40｜color on silk, hanging scroll

2 **秋映花器**｜三代 伊東陶山｜昭和41｜陶器・釉薬
   Flower Vase: Autumn Glow｜ITO Tozan III｜1966｜ceramic, glaze

3 **花籃「秋風」**｜柳下昌玕｜昭和42｜竹
   Flower Basket: Autumn Breeze｜YANAGISHITA Shokan｜1967｜bamboo

江戸時代中期から250年続く清水焼の名陶、清水六兵衞。六代六兵衞は、伝統を引き継ぎながら、新しい焼成や釉薬、絵付けの技法の開発に勤しみ、清水焼に革新をもたらしました。日本画の素養も身につけた作家で、本作のように洗練された構図の作品を多く残しています。金銀のきらびやかな釉薬に、ざらざらとした表面の肌理が滋味を与えています。

The Kiyomizu-yaki lineage of ceramicists, Kiyomizu Rokubei, traces back 250 years to the mid-Edo Period. While taking on the succession of the family's heritage, Kiyomizu Rokubei VI has put his energy into new techniques of firing, and refining methods of decorative painting to bring about innovations in Kiyomizu-style ceramics. This artist has familiarized himself with Japanese-style painting, and has produced many works of sophisticated designs such as this one. The gritty surface of the piece enhances the exquisiteness of the glittering gold and silver glaze.

古稀彩弦月壷│六代 清水六兵衞│昭和48│陶器・釉薬
Jar with Waning Moon Design│KIYOMIZU Rokubei VI│1973│ceramic, glaze

1

3

2

1 　くりとかたつむり｜長谷川 潔｜昭和25｜紙、エッチング
　　Chestnuts and a Snail｜HASEGAWA Kiyoshi｜1950｜paper, etching

2 　**稲穂蒔絵六角香合**｜迎田秋悦｜昭和3｜木・漆・金、蒔絵
　　Hexagonal Incense Case of Rice Ears Design, Maki-e｜KODA Shuetsu｜1928｜wood, lacquer, gold, maki-e

3 　**棗「稲」**｜白山松哉｜［不詳］｜木胎・金、蒔絵
　　Tea Caddy: Rice Plant｜SHIRAYAMA Shosai｜[n. d.]｜wood, lacquer, gold, maki-e

田人｜小川千甕｜昭和3｜紙本、着色、二曲一隻屏風
People Working in the Rice Field｜OGAWA Sen'yo｜1928｜color on paper, two-panels folding screen

白川女｜神阪松濤｜明治末｜絹本、着色、軸
Shirakawame (Woman from Shirakawa Selling Flowers)｜
KAMISAKA Shoto｜c. 1900-12｜color on silk, hanging scroll

1

3

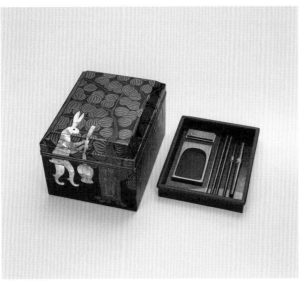

2

1 　能の女 井筒 ｜ 中堂憲一 ｜ 平成 2 ｜ 布、型染、額
　Female Figure of Noh Play "Izutsu" ｜ CHUDO Ken'ichi ｜ 1990 ｜ cloth, stencil dyed, framed

2 　しの田の森の秋宵 ｜ 加藤宗巌 ｜ 昭和 56 ｜ 銅、鍍銀・金彩
　Autumn Evening in Shinoda Forest (Scene from the Folklore "Shinoda-zuma") ｜ KATO Sogan ｜ 1981 ｜ copper, silver impregnation, gold paint

3 　月象之図 硯付手箱 ｜ 神坂祐吉 ｜ ［不詳］ ｜ 木・漆・貝、螺鈿
　Letter Box with Design: Hare in the Moon ｜ KAMISAKA Yukichi ｜ [n. d.] ｜ wood, lacquer, shell, raden inlay

晩秋

旧暦九月・新暦十月・長月

《寒露》　新暦十月八日頃

秋の虫がなく

《霜降》　新暦十月二十三日頃

葉が色づき始める

虫たちが名残を惜しむように鳴く秋の暮れ。朝晩の気温も低くなり、草葉に降りた露も冷えていきます。この季節に花ひらくのが、日本人にとって馴染み深い花である菊。毎年、京都府立植物園や泉涌寺などでは菊花展が催され、丹精こめて育てられたとりどりの菊が競艶します。ウィーンでデザインを学んだ上野リチ・リックスのプリントデザインは、菊花の連続模様でありながらも、手描きによって一花一花に微妙な違いを持たせることで、妙味を醸しだしています。

京都へ都が移されたのは七九四年十月二十二日のこと。この日を記念して行われるのが「時代祭」です。生きた時代絵巻と称されるこの祭りでは、明治維新から平安までの各時代の装束を身にまとった二千名の人々が市中を練り歩きます。祭りが終わり、洛北からちらほらと紅葉の便りが届くころ、洛西では柿が食べごろを迎えます。西京区大枝では道沿いにたくさんの直売所が並び、柿街道が作られます。

LATE AUTUMN

9th Month under Japanese lunisolar calendar | October | *NAGATSUKI*

KANRO
[Cold Dew]

October 8th
Autumn insects are chirping.

SOKO
[Frost Falls]

October 23rd
Leaves are coloring.

As autumn comes to a close, the insects' cries resound as if ruing the vestiges of the season. The dew falling on the grasses' leaves turns cold. The flower that blooms in this season is the chrysanthemum, so familiar to Japanese. Annual chrysanthemum exhibits are held at the Kyoto Botanical Garden and Sennyuji temple, where many types of chrysanthemums that have been lovingly raised vie to show their splendor. The print design by Felice "Lizzi" Rix-Ueno, who studied design in Vienna, imparts a refined beauty by creating subtle differences in each flower drawn by hand within the repetitive pattern of chrysanthemum flowers.

Kyoto became the capital on October 22, 794. The Jidai Matsuri (Festival of the Ages) is held on this day in commemoration of that day. Called a living period scroll painting, some 2,000 participants process through the city dressed in period costume from the Heian Period to the Meiji Restoration. After this festival, when word of the fall foliage comes from the northern region, persimmons reach their peak in the western part of Kyoto. Fruit stands line the streets of Oe in Nishikyo Ward, forming a persimmon highway.

プリント・デザイン「菊（白黒）」 | 上野リチ・リックス
Print Design: Chrysanthemum (Black and White) | Felice "Lizzi" RIX-UENO

晩秋 | LATE AUTUM

1

2

1　**ダリア** | 池田洛中 | 大正14頃 | 絹本、着色、額
　Dahlias | IKEDA Rakuchu | c. 1925 | color on silk, framed

2　**プリント・デザイン「菊（白黒）」** | 上野リチ・リックス |
　昭和15-20 | 紙、インク・鉛筆
　Print Design: Chrysanthemum (Black and White) |
　Felice "Lizzi" RIX-UENO | 1940-45 | paper, ink, pencil

3　**友禅菊華文振袖** | 三代 田畑喜八 | 大正末頃 | 絹、友禅
　Long-sleeved Kimono with Chrysanthemum Design | TABATA Kihachi III |
　c. 1925 | silk, yuzen dyed

檜垣の前に、大輪の菊が咲きほこっています。花弁が上方にカールして鱗のように重なる奥州菊は、数ある中でもひときわ華やかな品種。葉の部分がところどころ染め抜かれて洒脱な印象を与えます。作者の三代田畑喜八は、江戸時代後期に創業された京友禅の名跡の三代目。竹内栖鳳らに師事して日本画を学び、写実的でやわらかな趣をもつ染織作品を完成させました。その下絵図は、今でも多くの作家の手本となっています。

Large chrysanthemums bloom profusely in front of a woven cypress fence. With their petals that curl upward and layer upon each other like fish scales, Oshu chrysanthemums are among the showiest variety. Here and there the leaves are left undyed, giving an unconstrained effect. Tabata Kihachi III is the third generation of Kyo-yuzen masters tracing back to the end of the Edo Period. Studying under Takeuchi Seiho and other Japanese-style painters, he has perfected dyed works that are naturalistic and soft in tone. His design sketches continue to be used as examples by artists.

3

鵞鳥｜森 寛斎｜明治時代｜絹本、着色、軸
Goose ｜ MORI Kansai ｜
1868-1912 ｜ color on silk, hanging scroll

3

1

4

2

1 **葉鶏頭図花瓶**｜安藤十兵衛｜明治〜大正時代｜金属・釉薬、有線七宝(一対)
Flower Vases with Amaranthus Tricolor｜ANDO Jubei｜1868-1926｜metal, glaze, wired cloisonné, pair of vases

2 **七宝菊文煙草入**｜並河靖之｜明治後期｜金属・釉薬、有線七宝
Cigarette Case with Chrysanthemum Design｜NAMIKAWA Yasuyuki｜c. 1885-1912｜metal, glaze, wired cloisonné

3 **菊花図花瓶**｜香川勝廣｜明治時代｜銀、打出・象嵌(金・四分一)
Flower Vase with Chrysanthemum Deisgn｜KAGAWA Katsuhiro｜1868-1912｜silver, hammered, inlay (gold, shibuichi copper alloy)

4 **吹墨色絵菊花文飾壺**｜加藤土師萌｜昭和38頃｜陶器・釉薬、色絵
Ornamental Jar with Chrysanthemum Design, Overglaze Enamels with Misty Patterns｜KATO Hajime｜c. 1968｜ceramic, glaze, overglaze enamels

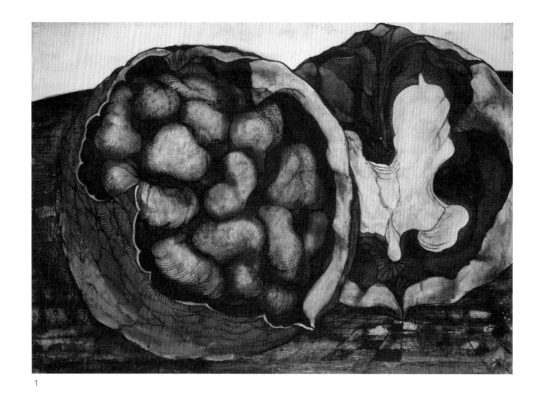

1

1 くるみ｜下村良之介｜昭和25｜紙本、着色、額
Walnut｜SHIMOMURA Ryonosuke｜
1950｜color on paper, framed

2 8つのくるみ｜浜口陽三｜昭和52｜紙、リトグラフ
Eight Walnuts｜HAMAGUCHI Yozo｜1977｜paper, lithograph

2

1

2

1 **柘榴に葡萄**｜小林清親｜［不詳］｜紙、木版
Pomegranates and Grapes｜KOBAYASHI Kiyochika｜[n. d.]｜paper, woodblock print

2 **柘榴染付壷**｜近藤悠三｜昭和50頃｜磁器・釉薬、染付
Vase with Pomegranate Design, Blue Underglaze｜KONDO Yuzo｜c. 1975｜porcelain, glaze, blue underglaze

1

2

1 **海幸**｜竹内栖鳳｜昭和14｜絹本、着色、額
Mackerels and Prawns｜TAKEUCHI Seiho｜1939｜color on silk, framed

2 **糸目菊絵椀**｜北大路魯山人｜昭和19頃｜木胎・漆
Covered Bowls with Chrysanthemum Design｜KITAOJI Rosanjin｜c.1944｜wood, lacquer

うづまさ牛祭｜冨田渓仙｜
大正9｜絹本、着色、軸（双幅）
Ox Festival at Koryu-ji Temple in Uzumasa｜
TOMITA Keisen｜1920｜
color on silk, hanging scrolls (diptych)

1　**童女と菊花**｜岸田劉生｜大正9｜紙、木版
　Young Girl and Chrysanthemums｜KISHIDA Ryusei｜1920｜paper, woodblock print

2　**朱菊盤**｜呉藤友乗｜昭和38｜木胎・漆
　Red Chrysanthemum-shaped Tray｜GOTO Yujo｜1963｜wood, lacquer

3　**蝶菊花文香合**｜六角紫水｜［不詳］｜木・漆・金・銀、蒔絵
　Incense Case with Chrysanthemum and Butterfly Design｜ROKKAKU Shisui｜[n. d.]｜wood, lacquer, gold, silver, maki-e

4　**菊文蒔絵棗**｜白山松哉｜明治～大正時代｜木・漆・金、蒔絵
　Tea Caddy with Chrysanthemum Design, Maki-e｜SHIRAYAMA Shosai｜1868-1923｜wood, lacquer, gold, maki-e

霜降 | SOKO [Frost Falls]

蔦もみじ｜久保田米僊｜明治18｜絹本、着色、軸
Ivy Turning into Yellow and Red｜KUBOTA Beisen｜
1885｜color on silk, hanging scroll

秋の驚異 ｜ 北脇 昇 ｜ 昭和20頃 ｜ 画布、油彩、額
Wonder in Autumn ｜ KITAWAKI Noboru ｜ c. 1945 ｜ oil on canva, framed

1

2

1 **洛北八瀬の秋**｜梅原龍三郎｜明治40｜板、油彩、額
Autumn in Yase, the Northern Suburbs of Kyoto｜
UMEHARA Ryuzaburo｜1907｜oil on board, framed

2 **等持院秋庭**｜新井謹也｜明治43｜板、油彩、額
Autumn Garden of Toji-in Temple｜ARAI Kin'ya｜
1910｜oil on board, framed

大原女図｜冨田渓仙｜大正15｜絹本、着色、軸
Oharame (Woman Peddlers from Ohara)｜
TOMITA Keisen｜1926｜color on silk, hanging scroll

加藤源之助は浅井忠に学んだ水彩画家で、京都の暮らしを柔らかな筆致
で描きだしました。本作は、頭上に柴をのせた大原女たちが三条大橋を
歩いている様子を描いたもの。寒くなる時期に備えて、暖をとるための
燃料を売りにきたのでしょう。今では特別な行事を別にして、その姿を
見ることはありませんが、大原や八瀬から頭に荷物をのせてやってくる
大原女は、京都の風物として古くより愛されてきました。

A watercolorist who studied under Asai Chu, Kato Gen'nosuke drew scenes from
life in Kyoto with a soft touch. This work depicts several Oharame women carrying
bundles of brushwood on their heads as they walk over the Sanjo Ohashi Bridge. They
have come to sell firewood for warmth as the season turns cold. Nowadays we can only
see them at special events, but in days of old Oharame women who came from Ohara
and Yase carrying goods on their heads were beloved as features of Kyoto.

三条大橋｜加藤源之助｜明治37｜紙、水彩、額
Sanjo Ohashi Bridge｜KATO Gen'nosuke｜1904｜paper, watercolor, framed

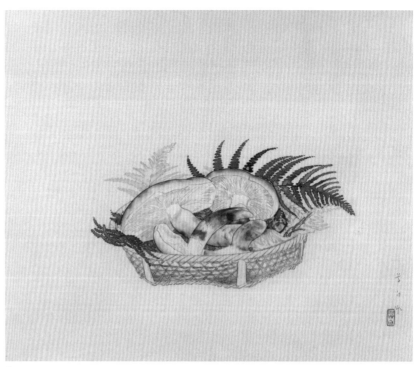

1

3

2

1 **松茸図**│伊藤草白│昭和初期│紙本、着色、軸
  Matsu-take Mushrooms│ITO Sohaku│c. 1926-40│color on paper, hanging scroll

2 **柿 牙彫置物**│安藤緑山│大正～昭和初│象牙、彫刻・着色
  Carved Ivory Figurine of Kakis│ANDO Ryokuzan│c. 1912-30│ivory, carved, dyed

3 **龍眼柿香盒**│船越春珉│昭和11│銅、鋳造
  Kaki-shaped Incense Case│FUNAKOSHI Shunmin│1936│copper, casting

2

1

3

1　**朱銅花瓶「晩秋」**｜高村豊周｜昭和46｜銅
　　Copper Red Flower Vase: Late Autumn｜TAKAMURA Toyochika｜1971｜copper

2　**柿釉壺**｜清水卯一｜昭和38｜陶器・釉薬
　　Jar, Reddish-brown Glaze｜SHIMIZU Uichi｜1963｜ceramic, glaze

3　**柿釉金彩鉢**｜石黒宗麿｜昭和43｜陶器・釉薬、金彩
　　Bowl, Reddish-brown Glaze with Gold Paint｜ISHIGURO Munemaro｜1968｜ceramic, glaze, gold paint

1

2

1 **鶉**｜井上永悠｜昭和30頃｜紙本、墨画淡彩、軸
　Quail｜INOUE Eiyu｜c. 1955｜sumi ink and tint color on paper, hanging scroll

2 **鶉文金彩壺**｜北原千鹿｜昭和13｜黄銅、鍛造・彫金
　Jar with Quail Design in Gold｜KITAHARA Senroku｜1938｜brass, wrought, carved

3 **ある晩秋の日**｜中野弘彦｜平成10｜紙本、着色、額
　A Day in Late Autumn｜NAKANO Hirohiko｜1998｜color on paper, framed

4 **霙降る夜**｜黒田 暢｜昭和51｜布、型染、額
　Sleeting Night｜KURODA Toru｜1976｜cloth, stencil dyed, framed

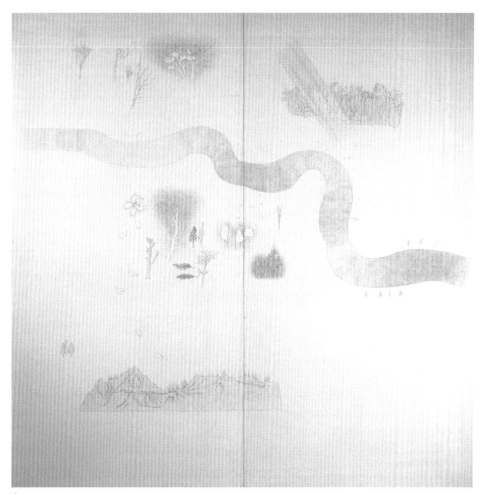

3

4

初冬

旧暦十月・新暦十一月・神無月

《立冬》

　　新暦十一月七日頃

　　大地が凍り始める

《小雪》

　　新暦十月二十二日頃

　　北風が木の葉を散らす

十一月に入って日差しが徐々に弱くなる冬の入り口。少しずつ冷え込む気温と反比例するように、京都の街には人が溢れていきます。人々のお目当ては、赤や黄に色づく紅葉。貴船や大原といった北の樹々から色づき始め、十一月下旬から十二月上旬には洛中一体が燃えるような赤や黄色に染め上げられます。各所で夜間拝観が行われ、灯りに照らし出された幽美な紅葉を堪能することができます。

十一月二十五日は、南座で恒例の「まねき上げ」が行われる日。太くうねった勘亭流で書かれた歌舞伎役者の看板が、劇場正面に掲げられます。この光景を境に、京都もいよいよ年の暮れの表情に。織田一磨の《京都風景：加茂川》は、この時期の哀愁ただよう風情を巧みに捉えています。寂びしい色合いの中で、川をのぞく舞妓さんの薄雪のようなうなじがいっそう目をひきます。織田は他にも、江戸や明治の面影が残る都市風景を版画で多く描いています。

EARLY WINTER

10th Month under Japanese lunisolar calendar | November | KANNAZUKI

RITTO
[Beginning of Winter]

November 7th
The ground starts to freeze.

SHOSETSU
[Lesser Snow]

November 22nd
North wind is scattering leaves.

In November the sunlight gradually weakens as winter approaches. As if in inverse proportion to the coming cold, people crowd the streets of Kyoto. They are in pursuit of the red and yellow of the fall foliage. The colors first tinge the trees in Kibune and Ohara in the north, and in late November to early December the entire city becomes tinted in blazing reds and yellows. Evening light-ups allow enjoyment of the delicate beauty of foliage lit against the night sky.

On November 25th, the list of plays and actors for the year-end Kabuki performances is displayed at Minami-za. The thick calligraphy sign noting the actors is set at the front of the theater. This is the signal that Kyoto is heading into the end of the year. Oda Kazuma's *Kyoto Scenes: Kamo River* expertly captures the melancholy of the scene. Amid the somber coloring, our eyes are drawn particularly to the light snow-like nape of the neck of the *maiko* peering down at the river. Oda has depicted in his woodblock prints other cityscapes that retain images from the Edo and Meiji Periods of the nineteenth century.

京都風景：加茂川 ｜ 織田一磨
Kyoto Scenes: Kamo River ｜ ODA Kazuma

1

洋画を学んだ後に、日本画へ転向した吹田草牧。それまでの日本画の表現を刷新するかのように、色鮮やかで濃密な風景画を多く描きました。本作で描かれているのは、豊臣秀吉が設計に携わった醍醐寺の三宝院庭園。桃山様式の豪華な庭園で、秀吉が「醍醐の花見」を催したことから現在でも桜の名所として有名ですが、紅葉の季節にも春に引けを取らない目映い景色を見せてくれます。

After studying Western-style painting, Suita Soboku reverted to Japanese-style painting. As if to renew the expressions of Japanese-style painting of the past, he painted many colorful and dense landscapes. This is the garden at Sanboin, within Daigo-ji Temple which Toyotomi Hideyoshi had a hand in designing. A sumptuous garden in the Momoyama style, it is renowned for its cherry blossoms from the time when Hideyoshi held his Flower Viewing at Daigo. But the blazing colors of the fall foliage season is no less a sight.

2

1 　**栂尾紅葉**　｜　川西 英　｜　昭和14　｜　紙、木版
　Red Leaves in Toganoo　｜　KAWANISHI Hide　｜　1939　｜　paper, woodblock print

2 　**醍醐寺泉庭**　｜　吹田草牧　｜　昭和3　｜　絹本、着色、二曲一隻屏風
　Garden of Daigo-ji Temple　｜　SUITA Soboku　｜　1928　｜　color on silk, two-panels folding screen

1　**白雲紅樹**｜都路華香｜大正3頃｜絹本、着色、軸
White Clouds over Red Leaves｜TSUJI Kako｜c. 1914｜color on silk, hanging scroll

2　**雲錦手大鉢**｜北大路魯山人｜昭和33｜陶器・釉薬、金彩
Large Bowl with Cherry-blossoms and Maple Trees Design｜KITAOJI Rosanjin｜1958｜ceramic, glaze, gold paint

初冬｜徳力富吉郎｜昭和3｜絹本、着色、二曲一隻屏風
Early Winter ｜ TOKURIKI Tomikichiro ｜ 1928 ｜ color on silk, two-panels folding screen

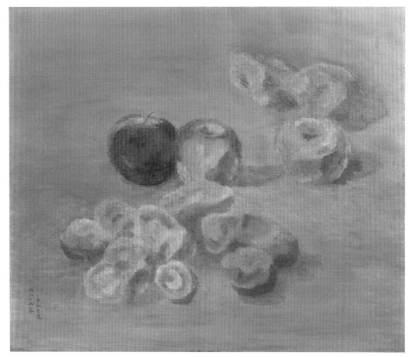

1

3

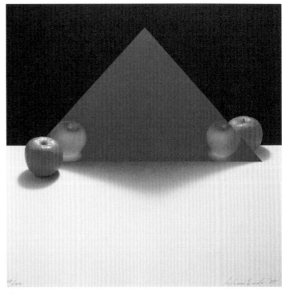

2

1 **林檎と馬鈴薯** │ 坂本繁二郎 │ 昭和15 │ 画布、油彩、額
   Apples and Potatoes │ SAKAMOTO Hanjiro │ 1940 │ oil on canvas, framed

2 **Space & Space (Apple IV)** │ 遠藤 享 │ 昭和60 │ 紙、オフセット・リトグラフ
   Space & Space (Apple IV) │ ENDO Susumu │ 1985 │ paper, offset, lithograph

3 **エヴァからもらった大きなリンゴ** │ 堀内正和 │ 昭和41 │ 合金・大理石
   Large Apple from Eva │ HORIUCHI Masakazu │ 1966 │ alloy, marble

1

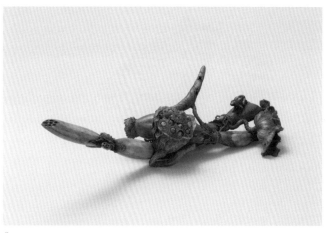

3

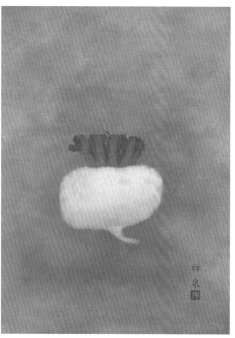

1 **型染立樹文着物**｜芹沢銈介｜昭和43｜木綿紬、型染
  Kimono with Standing Tree Design｜SERIZAWA Keisuke｜
  1968｜cotton pongee , stencil dyed

2 **蕪**｜徳岡神泉｜昭和33｜紙本、着色、額
  Turnip｜TOKUOKA Shinsen｜1958｜color on paper, framed

3 **蓮根に蛙 牙彫置物**｜石川光明｜明治時代｜象牙、彫刻・着色
  Carved Ivory Figurine of Lotus Root with Frog｜ISHIKAWA Komei｜
  1868-1912｜ivory, carved, dyed

2

1

2

1 **色葉**｜今井憲一｜昭和16｜画布、油彩、額
Colored Leaves｜IMAI Ken'ichi｜1941｜oil on canvas, framed

2 **石蕗図螺鈿蒔絵煙草箱**｜神坂雪佳（案）、神坂祐吉（作）｜明治末～大正初期｜木・漆・金・貝、蒔絵・螺鈿
Cigarette Box with Japanese Silver Leaf Design, Maki-e and Raden Inlay｜
KAMISAKA Sekka (design), KAMISAKA Yukichi (lacquerware)｜c. 1910-20｜wood, lacquer, gold, shell, maki-e and raden inlay

兎は野山に年中いますが、季語としては冬を表します。兎狩りが冬に行われることや、冬に真っ白に生え変わる毛が、雪を彷彿とさせることに由来するのでしょう。イギリスの陶芸家、バーナード・リーチは、そんな兎の躍動感溢れる姿を皿に焼き付けました。10年ほど日本に住んで白樺派や民藝運動の作家たちと交流していたリーチは、日英両国の技法を取り入れて、素朴であたたかみを感じさせる独自の作風を確立しました。

Rabbits live all year round in the fields and hills, but they are associated with winter. No doubt this derives from rabbit-hunting that takes place in winter, and from rabbit fur which turns white in winter which is reminiscent of snow. British ceramicist Bernard Leach fired onto a plate the figure of a rabbit full of lively motion. Leach lived in Japan some ten years and became familiar with the artists and writers of the Shirakabaha (White Birch Society) and the Mingei (Japanese Folk Arts) movement. Combining techniques from both Japan and Britain he developed his unique creative style that evokes simplicity and warmth.

楽焼大皿「兎」｜バーナード・リーチ｜大正9｜陶器・釉薬
Large Raku Ware Dish: Rabbit｜Bernard LEACH｜1920｜ceramic, glaze

京都風景：加茂川 ｜ 織田一磨 ｜ 大正14 ｜ 紙、リトグラフ
Kyoto Scenes: Kamo River ｜ ODA Kazuma ｜ 1925 ｜ paper, lithograph

1

4

3

2

1　**曲水**｜麻田辨自｜昭和44｜紙本、着色、二曲一隻屏風
　　Curving Stream｜ASADA Benji｜1969｜color on paper, two-panels folding screen

2　**木菟香炉**｜香取秀真｜昭和23｜青銅、鋳造
　　Horned Owl-shaped Incense Burner｜KATORI Hozuma｜1948｜bronze, casting

3　**みみずく香炉**｜香取秀真｜昭和28｜青銅、鋳造・象嵌（金）
　　Horned Owl-shaped Incense Burner｜KATORI Hozuma｜1953｜bronze, casting, inlay (gold)

4　**碧釉木兎文鉢**｜加藤土師萌｜昭和36｜陶器・釉薬
　　Bowl with Horned Owls Design, Cobalt Glaze｜KATO Hajime｜1961｜ceramic, glaze

1

2

1 **紬織着物「冬樹」**｜志村ふくみ｜昭和36｜絹糸・渋木・藍、紬織
  Pongee Kimono: Winter Tree｜SHIMURA Fukumi｜
  1961｜silk, bay berry, indigo, pongee weaving

2 **花器「稜」**｜加藤 鈔｜昭和39｜陶器・釉薬
  Flower Vase: Ridge｜KATO Sho｜1964｜ceramic, glaze

3 **枯野の狐**｜竹内栖鳳｜明治30｜絹本、着色、軸
  Fox in Desolate Field｜TAKEUCHI Seiho｜
  1897｜color on silk, hanging scroll

3

仲冬　旧暦十一月・新暦十二月・霜月

《大雪》

新暦十二月七日頃

冬雲が空を覆う

《冬至》

新暦十二月二十一日頃

雪の下で麦が伸びる

南天の赤い実がなり、比叡山の頂がうっすらと雪で覆われるころ、京都の街にも本格的な冬が到来します。大原に住んで自給自足の生活をしていた画家、小松均の《もや》は、羊歯や笹、南天、カラスウリが忍びやかに群生する様を、大胆な構図と細密な描写で表しています。

十二月八日は「事納め」。古くから農作業を終える日とされてきましたが、他の仕事も仕舞い時です。法輪寺ではこの日に、折れたり錆びたりした針をこんにゃくに挿して納める「針供養」が行われます。裁縫などの仕事に携わる人々が、針をねぎらい、技芸の上達を祈願する儀式です。五日後の十三日は「事始め」。お正月の準備が始まります。京都の人々にとって大事な準備のひとつが「大福梅」の授与。北野天満宮の境内で採れた梅をいただき、元旦の朝に茶や白湯に入れて飲むと、一年間の無病を祈願することができます。錦市場でおせちの食材を揃えて、新しい年をお迎えしましょう。

MID-WINTER

11th Month under Japanese lunisolar calendar | December | SHIMOTSUKI

TAISETSU
[Greater Snow]

December 7th
Winter cloud is covering the sky.

TOJI
[Winter Solstice]

December 21st
Wheat is growing under the snow.

When the nandina berries ripen red and the top of Mt. Hiei is dusted with snow, winter arrives in Kyoto. *Haze* by Komatsu Hitoshi, a painter who lived a self-sufficient life in Ohara, depicted with a bold composition and fine drawing how the fern, bamboo grass, nandina, and snake gourd stealthily grow together.

December 8th is the day for finishing work for the year. From olden times it was considered the end of farming for the year, but this is also the time when other work is completed. At Horinji this day is the memorial for old and broken sewing needles by piercing those needles into the gelatinous block made from devil's tongue starch. People in the sewing trades show thanks to their needles and pray to improve their skills. Five days later, on December 13th, it is the start of work day, when preparations for the New Year begin. For the people of Kyoto an important task is to acquire a plum of great fortune, Daifuku Ume. By receiving the plum from the trees on the grounds of Kitano Tenmangu and putting it into tea or hot water to drink on New Year's Day, they can pray for a year without illness. New Year's foods are sold in Nishiki Market to prepare to welcome in the New Year.

もや｜小松 均
Haze｜KOMATSU Hitoshi

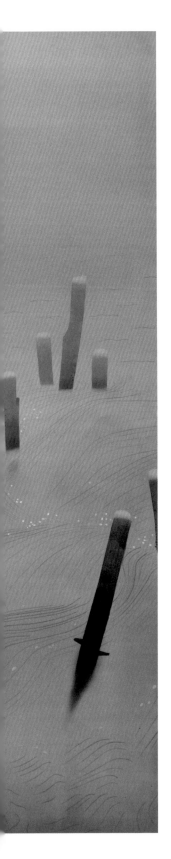

20代後半より優れた日本画を発表し始めた堂本印象。その仏画や花鳥画は、日本画の繊細さや華麗さを極めた表現として高く評価されました。本作は、冬が本格的に到来したころの川辺の様子を描いたもの。雪よりも純白な羽毛を持つ7羽の鷺が、寒さを凌ぐように身を寄せ合っています。川の遠景を霞ませることで広漠な空間が生まれており、冬の冷気がこちらまで流れ込んでくるかのような錯覚に襲われます。

In his latter twenties, Domoto Insho began to create gifted paintings in the Japanese style. His Buddhist and bird-and-flower paintings were highly praised as expressing the height of delicacy and beauty of Japanese-style painting. This work depicts the scene of a riverside just as the full force of winter arrives. Seven herons with feathers whiter than snow huddle together as if to ward off the chill air. By covering the river with mist an expansive space is created, giving the illusion that the cold winter air may be flowing toward us.

冬朝｜堂本印象｜昭和7｜絹本、着色、額
Winter Morning｜DOMOTO Insho｜1932｜color on silk, framed

2

1

1　もや｜小松 均｜昭和5｜紙本、着色、二曲一双屏風
　　Haze｜KOMATSU Hitoshi｜1930｜color on paper, pair of two-panels folding screens

2　紅葉・雪中之景図｜［不詳］｜明治11-44｜天鵞絨、友禅
　　Scenes of Red Leaves and Snow｜[Unknown]｜1879-1911｜velvet, yuzen dyed

蔬菜｜小林古径｜昭和18｜紙本、着色、額
Vegetables｜KOBAYASHI Kokei｜1943｜color on paper, framed

野菜｜須田国太郎｜昭和15頃｜画布、油彩、額
Vegetables｜SUDA Kunitaro｜c. 1940｜oil on canvas, framed

1

3

2

4

1　京都風景:清水寺｜織田一磨｜大正14｜紙、リトグラフ
Kyoto Scenes: Kiyomizu-dera Temple ｜ ODA Kazuma ｜ 1925 ｜ paper, lithograph

2　萩焼茶碗「看雪」｜十五代 樂吉左衞門｜平成27｜陶器・釉薬
Hagi Ware Teabowl: Snow Scene Viewing ｜ RAKU Kichizaemon XV ｜ 2015 ｜ ceramic, glaze

3　染付花瓶「風雪」｜松風栄一｜［不詳］｜磁器・釉薬
Flower Vase, Blue and White: Wind and Snow ｜ SHOFU Eiichi ｜ [n. d.] ｜ porcelain, glaze

4　雪｜野島康三｜昭和17｜ゼラチン・シルバー・プリント
Snow ｜ NOJIMA Yasuzo ｜ 1942 ｜ gelatin silver print

雪の中の馬 ｜ 鈴木 治 ｜ 昭和48 ｜ 陶器・釉薬
Horse in the Snow ｜ SUZUKI Osamu ｜ 1973 ｜ ceramic, glaze

1

2

1　**竹に雀図七宝花瓶**｜安藤十兵衛｜明治～大正時代｜金属・釉薬、有線七宝（一対）
　Cloisonné Flower Vases with Bamboo and Sparrows Design｜ANDO Jubei｜1868-1926｜metal, glaze, wired cloisonné, pair of vases

2　**染付花鳥花入**｜北大路魯山人｜昭和14頃｜磁器・釉薬、染付
　Flower Vase with Flower and Bird Design, Blue Underglaze｜KITAOJI Rosanjin｜c. 1939｜porcelain, glaze, blue underglaze

1

2

1 **南瓜** │ 井上永悠 │ 昭和30-34 │ 紙本、着色、額
Pumpkin │ INOUE Eiyu │ c. 1955-59 │ color on paper, framed

2 **蜜柑 牙彫置物** │ 安藤緑山 │ 大正～昭和初 │ 象牙、彫刻・着色
Carved Ivory Figurines of Japanese Mandarin │ ANDO Ryokuzan │ c. 1912-30 │ ivory, carved, dyed

露店｜三谷十糸子｜昭和4｜絹本、着色、二曲一隻屏風
Street Stall｜MITANI Toshiko｜1929｜color on silk, two-panels folding screen

五重塔で有名な東寺では、毎月21日に縁日が催されます。21日は弘法大師空海の月命日で、この日に参詣すると功徳があると言われます。12月の縁日は「終い弘法」とも呼ばれ、特に賑わう日。正月の縁起物や食材を売る露店が並びます。染色家の稲垣稔次郎は、戦後の型絵染の可能性を大きく拓いた人物で、洗練された形と複雑な色味で対象を表現します。本作の他にも年末の四条や年明けの西陣など、折々の京都の姿を染め上げました。

Famed for its five-tiered pagoda, Toji Temple holds a temple festival on the twenty-first of each month. That day is the memorial day for the founder of the sect, Kobo-Daishi Kukai. Worshipping at the temple on that day is said to accumulate blessings. The December fair is the last Kobo of the year, and is especially thronged with people. Stalls selling New Year amulets and foodstuffs line the grounds. Stencil-dye artist Inagaki Toshijiro was a major figure in promoting the possibilities of stencil-dyeing in postwar times. His works express the contrast between refined shapes and complex colors. In addition to this work, he has created dyed scenes of Kyoto through the seasons, such as Shijo at yearend and the New Year in Nishijin.

型染壁掛「東寺の縁日」｜稲垣稔次郎｜昭和27頃｜木綿、型染、額
Stencil Dyed Tapestry: Fair in To-ji Temple｜INAGAKI Toshijiro｜c. 1952｜cotton, stencil dyed, framed

晩冬

旧暦十二月・新暦一月・師走

《小寒》
新暦一月五日頃
寒の入りを迎える

《大寒》
新暦一月二十日頃
寒さが極まる

年が明けて、一年の中でもっとも寒さが極まるころ。森田子龍の《凍》の文字は、寒さでこわばる体を一思いに動かして書かれたかのようです。森田は、欧米の前衛芸術に触れて日本の書を革新した人物で、文字と抽象の境にあるような作品を残しています。

一月の京都は、新年を寿ぐ行事で華やぎます。とりわけ街を賑わすのが京都ゑびす神社の「ゑびす大祭」。商売繁昌や家運隆昌を祈願する祭りで、五日間にわたって餅つき神事や福笹の授与などが行われます。二月に入って、来るべき春を迎えるために行われるのが節分の行事です。季節の変わり目には悪い気が溜まりやすいとされることから、福豆をまいて邪気を祓います。吉田神社などでは節分祭が大々的に行われ、福豆を授かりにいく人たちで賑わいます。底冷えの厳しい時季ですが、参道に並ぶ屋台のあたたかな食べ物に、人々の顔も思わずほころびます。京都の冬もいよいよお仕舞いです。

LATE WINTER

12th Month under Japanese lunisolar calendar | January | *SHIWASU*

SHOKAN
[Lesser Cold]

January 5th
Coldest season is beginning.

DAIKAN
[Greater Cold]

January 20th
Coldness is peaking.

With the start of the New Year comes the most frigid time of the year. Morita Shiryu's calligraphy *Frozen* is written as if he were moving his body, stiffened in the cold, in one intense effort. Morita revolutionized Japanese calligraphy after his exposure to avant-garde art of the West, leaving works that explored the boundary between words and abstraction.

Kyoto in January is full of lively events celebrating the New Year. A particularly spirited event is the Ebisu Festival at Kyoto Ebisu Shrine to pray that businesses will prosper and families will thrive in the coming year. During the five-day festival, there are rice-cake pounding rites and offerings of bamboo branches adorned with amulets bringing fortune. In early February, the Setsubun Festival marks the coming spring. As it is thought that malaise tends to collect at the change of the seasons, dried beans are scattered to dispel the evil spirits. At Yoshida Shrine and other shrines the Setsubun Festival is a major event, thronged by people keen on having the beans scattered onto them. In this season of bone-chilling cold, the warm food offered in the stalls leading to the shrine causes people to smile. Kyoto's winter is about to come to an end.

凍 | 森田子龍
Frozen | MORITA Shiryu

晩冬 | LATE WINTER

小寒 | *SHOKAN* [Lesser Cold]

1

明治から昭和にかけて活躍した日本画家の麻田辨自。日本の風景や動植物を伝統的な技法で描きましたが、その構図や筆致には強烈な個性が宿っています。雪が降り積もった笹藪を歩くオスの雉を描いた本作では、朦朧と描かれた笹と、はっきりと塗られた雉が対照的に表されています。雉は春にメスを鳴いて探しますが、今はまだ雪深い季節。尾をピンと立てて、孤独に茂みをさすらいます。

Asada Benji was active from early to latter twentieth century. His drew Japanese landscapes and animals in a traditional technique, but his design and brushwork are infused with a fierce individuality. In this work featuring a male pheasant walking in a thicket of bamboo grass covered with snow, the indistinctly drawn bamboo grass and the clearly painted pheasant are contrasted. In the spring the male pheasant will call out to find a mate, but this season is still deep in snow. With his tail extended straight up, he wanders lonely in the thicket.

2

3

1 **暮雪**｜麻田辨自｜昭和55｜紙本、着色、額
Snow in the Evening｜ASADA Benji｜1980｜color on paper, framed

2 **鮒**｜新見虚舟｜昭和5｜絹本、着色、軸
Crucian Carps｜SHINMI Kyoshu｜1930｜color on silk, hanging scroll

3 **海鼠釉黒流描大鉢**｜浜田庄司｜昭和37｜陶器・釉薬
Large Bowl, Black Trails on Translucent Glaze｜HAMADA Shoji｜1962｜ceramic, glaze

友禅着物｜木村雨山｜昭和40代｜絹、友禅
Kimono, Yuzen Dyed｜KIMURA Uzan｜1965-75｜silk, yuzen dyed

静物｜野島康三｜昭和17｜ゼラチン・シルバー・プリント
Still Life｜NOJIMA Yasuzo｜1942｜gelatin silver print

葉ぼたんと現代少女｜谷角日沙春｜昭和24｜絹本、着色、軸
A Modern Girl with Ornamental Kale｜TANIKADO Hisaharu｜
1949｜color on silk, hanging scroll

1

2

1 **出町の冬** | 加藤源之助 | 明治39 | 紙、水彩、額
   Winter in Demachi | KATO Gen'nosuke | 1906 | paper, watercolor, framed

2 **雪の鞍馬** | 伊藤仁三郎 | 昭和35-44 | 紙、木版
   Snow in Kurama | ITO Nisaburo | 1960-69 | paper, woodblock print

2

1

3

側面までびっしりと南天の実と葉が描かれた、何とも豪勢な棚。冬景色に赤色をぽとぽとと点じていた南天も、そろそろ見ごろを終えます。作者は日本を代表する漆芸家、吉田源十郎。東京美術学校（現東京藝術大学）で漆芸を学び、その卓越した技術によって数々の賞を受けています。吉田の作品は技術的に優れているだけではなく、色調や構図においても先鋭的で、新しい時代の工芸を切り拓く嚆矢となりました。

Nandina berries and leaves cover even the side panels of this luxurious shelf. The height of viewing nandina which provided dots of red among the winterscape is about to end. Yoshida Genjuro was a leading Japanese lacquerware artist. He studied lacquer art at the Tokyo Fine Arts School (now Tokyo University of the Arts), receiving numerous awards for his superior technique. Not only are Yoshida's works superb in technique, they also show his radical coloring and design which make him a pioneer in formulating art and craft for a new age.

4

1 **呉須赤絵南天水指** | 河合卯之助 | ［不詳］ | 陶器・釉薬
Water Container with Nandina Design, Blue and Red Overglaze Enamels | KAWAI Unosuke | [n. d.] | ceramic, glaze

2 **黄瀬戸花入** | 荒川豊蔵 | 昭和42 | 陶器・釉薬
Yellow Seto Ware Flower Vase | ARAKAWA Toyozo | 1967 | ceramic, glaze

3 **南天棚** | 吉田源十郎 | 昭和11 | 木胎・漆・蒔絵
Shelf with Nandina Deisign | YOSHIDA Genjuro | 1936 | wood, lacquer, maki-e

4 **つれづれの日** | 千種掃雲 | 明治42 | 絹本、着色、額
A Tedious Day | CHIGUSA Soun | 1909 | color on silk, framed

1

2

1　**氷湖（小さい氷湖）**｜山口 薫｜昭和37｜画布、油彩、額
　Ice-bound Lake (Little Ice-bound Lake)｜YAMAGUCHI Kaoru｜1962｜oil on canvas, framed

2　**波濤図**｜四代 飯田新七｜明治43頃｜絹、刺繍、額
　Waves｜IIDA Shinshichi IV｜c. 1910｜silk, embroidery, framed

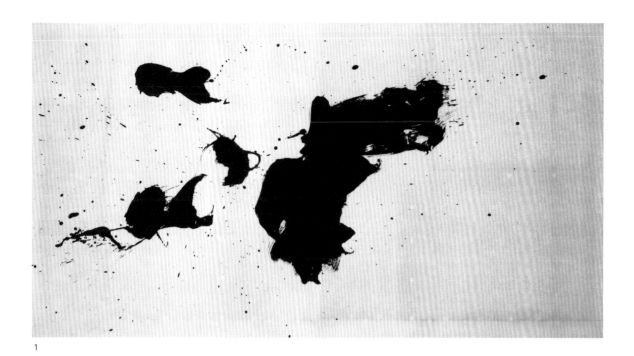

1

3

2

1 凍｜森田子龍｜昭和32｜紙・パネル、墨、額
  Frozen｜MORITA Shiryu｜1957｜paper, panel, sumi ink, framed

2 冬鏡｜大西 茂｜昭和30｜多重露光・フォトグラム
  Winter Mirror｜ONISHI Shigeru｜1955｜multiple exposure, photogram

3 凍結｜大西 茂｜昭和30｜多重露光・フォトグラム
  Frozen｜ONISHI Shigeru｜1955｜multiple exposure, photogram

正月

[The New Year]
SHOGATSU

明けましておめでとうございます。新しい一年の幕開けです。夜半から、お寺や神社は初詣の人々で賑わいます。なかでも元旦の風物詩となっているのが、御神火を縄に移して持ち帰る、八坂神社の「をけら詣り」。いただいた火で、神前の明かりを灯したり新年のお雑煮を炊いたりするのが習わしです。京都のお雑煮は白味噌仕立て。その朗らかな乳白色は、元旦の朝の澄んだ空気によく似合います。

初夢は正月の楽しみのひとつ。もっとも縁起が良い富士が現れるよう、富士の絵を見てはいかがでしょう。池田満寿夫が描いた《二重富士》は、本物の富士の後ろに、蜃気楼のような赤いシルエットが浮かんでいます。赤と金の配色が華々しく、右上りに棚引く雲にも勢いがあります。

三が日には八坂神社の「かるた始め式」や、下鴨神社の「蹴鞠はじめ」など新年を寿ぐ行事がさまざまに執り行われます。七日には七草粥で正月のご馳走で疲れた胃を休め、一年の息災を祈りましょう。

With New Year's greetings, the curtain rises on a brand new year. From New Year's Eve and into the New Year, temples and shrines are filled with people offering prayers for the coming year. An old custom that continues to this day is Yasaka Jinja Shrine's "Okera Mairi" festival. Worshippers receive a flame that lights the end of a rope and swirl it around to take home to light the lanterns on the family altar and to cook special New Year's soup. Kyoto's soup is made with white miso. The light milky color is a fitting accompaniment to the clear air of the New Year's Day morning.

One of the pleasures of the New Year is the first dream of the year. Gazing at a painting of Mt. Fuji might inspire one to have a dream with this most auspicious symbol. In Ikeda Masuo's *Double Image of Mt. Fuji* a mirage-like red silhouette floats behind the real Mt. Fuji. The red and gold coloration is spectacular and the clouds that flow toward the upper right show vigor.

During the first three days of the New Year, events celebrating the start of the year are held, with Yasaka Jinja Shrine's "first *karuta* card game," the poetry-matching card game, and Shimogamo Jinja Shrine's "first *kemari* game," the recreation of classic courtiers' kick ball game. On January 7, people rest their stomachs from the rich foods of the New Year celebrations by eating the seven grasses rice gruel and praying for a year of good health.

二重富士｜池田満寿夫
Double Image of Mt. Fuji｜IKEDA Masuo

二重富士｜池田満寿夫｜平成8｜紙、リトグラフ
Double Image of Mt. Fuji｜IKEDA Masuo｜1996｜paper, lithograph

1

2

1　**一陽来復**｜水越松南｜昭和23｜絹本、着色、軸
Winter Ends and Spring Arrives｜MIZUKOSHI Shonan｜
1948｜color on silk, hanging scroll

2　**朝陽磁鶴首花瓶**｜板谷波山｜昭和13｜磁器・釉薬
Flower Vase with Crane's Neck Shape Design, Copper Glaze｜
ITAYA Hazan｜1938｜porcelain, glaze

1

3

2

1　**獅子頭**｜熊谷守一｜昭和49｜板、油彩、額
　Head of Shishi (A Mask for Dance Dedicated to Gods)｜KUMAGAI Morikazu｜1974｜oil on board, framed

2　**獅子文小箱**｜清水南山｜昭和3｜赤銅・銅、鍛造・象嵌
　Small Casket with Shishi (Imaginary Lion) Design｜SHIMIZU Nanzan｜1928｜akagane, copper, wrought, inlay

3　**紅花緑葉獅子香盆**｜二十代 堆朱楊成｜大正8｜木・漆、彫漆
　Tray with Red Flower, Green Leaf and Shishi (Imaginary Lion) Design｜TSUISHU Yozei XX｜1919｜wood, lacquer, carved lacquer

2

3

1

1　老松孔雀図｜今尾景年｜大正5｜絹本、着色、軸
Old Pine and Peacocks｜IMAO Keinen｜1916｜color on silk, hanging scroll

2　孔雀置物｜長谷川一清｜明治時代｜木・銀・金
Figurines of Peacock｜HASEGAWA Issei｜1868-1912｜wood, silver, gold

3　三茄子 牙彫置物｜安藤緑山｜大正〜昭和初｜象牙、彫刻・着色
Carved Ivory Figurine of Three Eggplants｜ANDO Ryokuzan｜c. 1912-30｜ivory, carved, dyed

訪問着「夢」｜ 小倉建亮 ｜ 昭和39 ｜ 絹、絞染
Kimono: Dream ｜ OGURA Kensuke ｜ 1964 ｜ silk, tie dyed

仏手柑 牙彫置物｜安藤緑山｜大正〜昭和初｜象牙、彫刻・着色
Carved Ivory Figurine of Budda's Hand Citrons｜ANDO Ryokuzan｜c. 1912-30｜ivory, carved, dyed

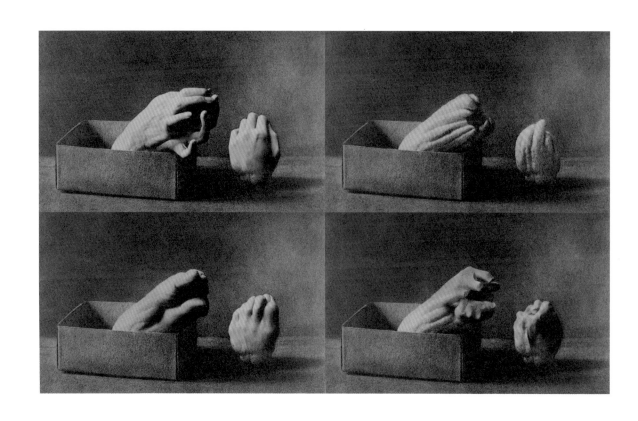

フィンガー・シュトロン（ノジマ）1 - 4 │ 森村泰昌 │ 平成2 │ カラー写真（4点組）
Fingered Citrons (Nojima) 1-4 │ MORIMURA Yasumasa │ 1990 │ color photographs (set of 4 prints)

京都国立近代美術館コレクションにみる二十四節気

池田祐子

与し、日本の芸術の近代化において重要な役割を果たしました。しかし政治の中心である東京で語られる日本の「近代美術史」において、それが十全に検証されているとは言えません。

そこで新しく京都に設置される国立近代美術館の使命のひとつが、明治維新以降の京都を中心とした芸術活動の検証とその作品収集におかれたことは、当然のことでした。また、「芸術産業」都市の京都にある美術館として、絵画や彫刻のようないわゆる純粋芸術だけではなく、工芸やデザインといった応用芸術、つまりより密接に暮らしと関わる分野の作品をも積極的に研究・収集していくという基本方針が立てられました。この二つの原則は、現在でも当館のあらゆる活動の基礎となっています。

一九六七年に、国立近代美術館京都分館は、京都国立近代美術館として念願の独立を果たしました。しかし開館時に京都市から譲渡された旧勧業館を再利用した美術館建物には、適切な収蔵庫もなく、コレクションを常時展示するスペースもありませんでした。先に述べた二つの基本方針に基づき、より充実した作品の収集・研究・展示活動ができるようになったのは、新美術館建物が開館してからのことになります。それから三十四年が経ち、現在では約一二、七〇〇点の作品・資料を収蔵しています。また4階のコレクション・ギャラリーでは、一年間におよそ五回の「コレクション展」を開催して、その都度約一五〇点の作品をさまざまな角度から紹介しています。

京都国立近代美術館とそのコレクション

京都国立近代美術館は、京都市中心部から鴨川を越えた東側の岡崎公園内にあります。向かいには日本で二番目の公立美術館として一九三三年に開館した京都市京セラ美術館があり、両者の間には平安神宮への入口となる朱塗りの大鳥居がそびえています。和洋折衷のいわゆる帝冠様式の京都市美術館建物とは対照的に、建築のノーベル賞と呼ばれるプリツカー賞を受賞した槇文彦設計により一九八六年に建てられた当館の建物は、ガラスやスチールに御影石を組み合わせたモダンなデザインですが、多用されているグリッドは障子や碁盤の目状の京都の市街地を連想させます。美術館建物4階には東に向かって大きな窓が設えられており、そこからは比叡山から将軍塚へと連なる東山が見渡せ、その四季折々の風景を愉しむことができます。そしてその4階には当館の所蔵作品を展示するコレクション・ギャラリーがあります。

京都国立近代美術館は、一九五二年に東京に開館した国立近代美術館の分館として、一九六三年に現在地に開館しました。京都への国立美術館の誘致は、フランス政府による松方コレクションの返還がきっかけでしたが、フランス政府が松方コレクションの首都東京での展示公開を返還条件としたため、叶いませんでした。そこで目指されたのが、京都での国立近代美術館の設置です。平安の昔から日本のみやこであった京都には、芸術に携わる数多くの人々が生活していました。明治維新に相応しい芸術のあり方を模索し、後進を育成しました。例えば、東京美術学校と京都市立絵画専門学校に先んじて開設された京都府画学校は、それが、後に京都市立美術工芸学校と京都市立絵画専門学校となり、現在の京都市立芸術大学へと繋がっています。京都高等工芸学校(現在の京都工芸繊維大学)を含むこのような学校組織だけではなく、日本画の画家たちによる画塾や洋画・水彩画を教授する関西美術院、さらには各種工芸の工房や団体の活発な活動も、近代京都の芸術制作を支えた重要な要素でした。そこから巣立った芸術家たちは、明治以降活発化する各種博覧会や展覧会にも積極的に関

コレクションにみる二十四節気

京都国立近代美術館のコレクションの最も大きな特徴は、それが幅広いジャンルにわたっていることです。列挙すると、日本画、油彩画、水彩画、版画、素描、彫刻、陶芸、漆芸、金工、木竹工、ガラス、染織、人形、写真となり、そこに、今列挙したジャンルの枠組みを越えていくような作品群「その他」や、作家の制作活動や芸術潮流を理解するために欠かせない「美術資料」が加わります。また、日本の作家のみならず、外国作家の作品も数多く所蔵していますが、それらは基本的に、日本(美術)との影響関係が指摘されうるかどうか、という観点から選ばれ、コレクションに加えられています。

「二十四節気」をテーマにコレクションから作品を選ぶにあたり、これら様々な

ジャンルを可能な限り網羅するようつとめました。その一方で、特定の季節に結び付けづらい作品や国外作家の作品の多くは、たとえ当館コレクションの代表的作品（例えばパブロ・ピカソ《静物─燭台、パレット、ミノタウロスの頭部》など）であってもここには含まれていませんが、「二十四節気」に注目することで、本書はいわゆる「所蔵作品名選」ではありません。そこには伝統的にくらしと密接な関係を結んできた日本画や工芸作品を中心に、当館コレクションの多彩さがより感じられる内容になっています。

「二十四節気」は、さらに「七十二候」に分けられます。ただ、旧暦と新暦の違いや、近年の気候温暖化も相まって、その内容は必ずしも私たちの実際の季節感とは一致しない部分もあります。そこで、作品選定について、各節気に沿いながら簡単にご説明することにしましょう。

I 立春

二十四節気最初の節気で、初めて春の気配が現れる季節です。ここには椿を主題にした作品を集めました。森野嘉光《緑釉窯変赤黒花瓶》では、緑の釉薬の上に赤い釉薬が拡がるさまを椿に見立てています。第一候「東風解凍（はるかぜこおりをとく）」にちなみ「春の雪」や「雪解け」を連想させる作品を加えました。新潟佐渡出身の土田麦僊による鮭の絵では、落款に「二月に写す」と記されており、この鮭がお正月の新巻鮭であることがうかがえます。

2 雨水

雪が雨に変わるころ、梅が盛りを迎えます。梅を主題にした作品に加え、第六候「草木萌動（そうもくめばえいずる）」を表現した作品を集めました。池田遥邨《春風》に描かれているのは宇治平等院辺りの風景です。川端弥之助も早春の風景として城南地域を主題にしています。また吉田白嶺と藤井達吉による《上代雛と雛屏風》は、当館が所蔵する唯一の雛人形です。

3 啓蟄

徐々に春めき、虫たちが動き始めるころに相応しく、蝶や蜥蜴を主題とした作品を選んでいます。この時期の花としては、桃の花やチューリップ、そして木瓜や木蓮を念頭におきながら作品を選んでいます。シンビジウムの鉢植えなどが描かれた野長瀬晩夏作品のタイトル《遅日》鳥かごやシンビジウムの鉢植えなどが描かれた野長瀬晩夏作品のタイトル《遅日》

4 春分

この日を境に、陽が延びていきます。彼岸には先祖のお墓参りをしますが、寺島紫明《彼岸》は、まさにその情景を切り取った作品。彼岸が終われば桜の季節です。中でも円山公園のしだれ桜は、多くの作家が好んで描いています。一方村上華岳《夜桜之図》の舞台は平野神社。画面をよく見ると「おでん」の文字。床机におかれた食べ物から、当時豆腐田楽をそう呼んでいたことがわかります。春が旬の食べ物として、同じく華岳が蝶や栄螺を描いた作品も加えました。

5 清明

「清浄明潔」にして春本番。引き続き桜を中心に、アザミやアネモネといった花を主題にした作品を選んでいます。名高い醍醐寺の桜の他にも、北野や栗田口、清水寺といった京都市内各所の春の風景を描いた作品を集めました。坂本繁二郎の優品からは、春の息吹が感じられる《母仔馬》を、そして春が旬の魚の主役「鯛」を描いた西村五雲《鮮魚》もここに加えています。

6 穀雨

農作物への恵みの春の雨。第十八候は「牡丹華（ぼたんはなさく）」。三代清風与平や五代清水六兵衛も、古陶磁研究の成果を発揮した作品で百花の王と呼ばれる牡丹を主題にしています。雨とともに成長するのが蔓をもつマメ科の植物。それを色絵で描いた河合卯之助の作品、螺鈿の技法で表現した池田泰真の漆の手箱を、さらに新緑を増す笹を表現した北村武資の経錦着物《笹の春》も加えました。

7 立夏

端午の節句の季節。冨田渓仙《浦嶋子図》や、まるで生きているように動く高瀬好山《鯉》は、それにちなんだ作品です。そして五月といえば、伊藤仁三郎が木版画の主題とした葵祭。祭列には御所車も登場します。主題となる植物は紫蘭や芥子、朴の花そして日本原産の藤の花など。第二十一候は「竹笋生（たけのこしょうず）」。牙彫の竹の子には梅の実が添えられています。茶道でも風炉となり、道具も夏らしいものに替わります。

209

8 小満

草木が成長して茂る頃、農家では田植えの準備が始まります。新緑が美しいこの季節、貴船神社では貴船祭が開催され、舞楽奉納や神輿巡行が行われます。陽気に誘われて、天道虫のような虫たちや蝸牛の動きも活発に。この季節の花は何といっても薔薇。明治維新以降に輸入された華やかな西洋原産の薔薇は、数多くの人々を魅了し、作品の主題となりました。またこの時期は麦の収穫期「麦秋」でもあります。

9 芒種

穀物の種をまく季節、梅雨が到来します。梅雨の花といえば紫陽花。河合卯之助が色絵で表現した京鹿の子は日本原産のバラ科植物です。また、この時期の果物として枇杷とさくらんぼそしてトマトを描いた作品を選んでいます。高瀬好山《蟷螂》は第二十五候「蟷螂生（かまきりしょうず）」にちなみ、そして福本潮子《夏着尺》もしび》は第二十七候「腐草為螢（くされたるくさほたるとなる）」の蛍の光に見立てました。

10 夏至

陽が最も長い時期。第二十九候「菖蒲華（あやめはなさく）」にちなんで安田靫彦の作品を選びました。四代清水六兵衞による花瓶のアール・ヌーヴォー風図案は萱草の花。橘や芹の花も巧みにデザイン化されています。そして千種掃雲《下鴨神社夏越神事》に見られるように、この時期人々は茅の輪をくぐって無病息災を祈ります。

11 小暑

新暦七月七日の七夕にちなんで『竹取物語』を主題にした作品を選びました。梅雨の終わりが近づき暑さが増していくこの頃、不動立山《夕立》に描かれた東本願寺の側溝のように、市内各所で蓮の花や睡蓮を目にします。その多様な表現を集めました。ほかには合歓の花や源氏物語にも登場する末摘花、そして夏野菜の胡瓜。ハンナ・ヘーヒ《日本の夏》は、一九七四年に当館で日本初の個展が開催された記念に寄贈された作品です。

12 大暑

夏の盛り、磯田又一郎《夏座敷》にはくらしの中に涼を求める工夫が見てとれます。屋外では木陰に憩い、氷を食べることで暑さをしのぐこともあります。見た目す。

13 立秋

に涼しげな金魚もこの季節ならでは。子供たちにとって夏休みのこの時期、海や兜虫を主題にした作品も加えました。旬の野菜としては、その形が特徴的な鹿ヶ谷南瓜。そして八月一日は八朔。芸舞妓が正装でお世話になっている方々にごあいさつにまわります。

「暑中お見舞い」が「残暑お見舞い」に替わるころ、旧暦の七夕が行われます。まだまだ暑いこの時期の植物として、向日葵や笹そして葛の花を主題とした作品を選びました。瓜を描いたり、象ったりした作品が多いのもこの季節の特徴です。同じく季節の食材として、安井曾太郎《桃》と安藤緑山による本物と見まごうばかりの《玉蜀黍 牙彫置物》を加えました。そして二代田辺竹雲斎の花入れの銘は、まさに《秋立つ》です。

14 処暑

ようやく暑さが峠を越える頃、街中のいたるところで軒先下まで成長した朝顔を見かけます。朝顔を撫子も木槿も、見た目涼やかながら夏の名残を感じさせる花々それらを主題にした作品を選んでいます。福田平八郎と深見陶治の作品タイトルである《清晨》は「すがすがしい朝」という意味。《初秋》と題された野島康三の写真作品からもその空気感が漂います。

15 白露

草花に朝露がつき始める季節、山口華楊《白露》は向日葵を主題にこの季節そのものを描いた作品。数ある所蔵作品の中でも、節気のいたるところで軒先下まで成長したものです。露草が描かれているのは池田遥邨《朧夜》。さらに秋の七草のひとつである萩や桔梗、鶏頭そして燃えるような曼珠沙華を主題にした作品も選びました。重陽の節句（菊花節）を主題としたのは近代美人画の名手鏑木清方。そしてこの時期、京都各地に鴨が飛来します。

16 秋分

これから陽が短くなっていきます。第四十八候「水始涸（みずはじめてかるる）」に従い、稲刈りの準備をする季節です。この頃に迎える仲秋の名月は、六代清水六兵衞《古稀彩弦月壷》や神坂祐吉《月象之図硯付手箱》で巧みに造形化されています。また秋は、浄瑠璃『信稲や秋風、そして秋の野を主題にした作品を選びました。

太妻』や能『井筒』の舞台でもあります。

17 寒露

冷たい露が降りる頃、五穀豊穣・悪魔退散を祈願して、京都の三大奇祭のひとつ、牛祭が広隆寺で開催されます。そして第五十候は「菊花開（きくのはなひらく）」。ここでは工芸作品を中心に菊を様々に表現した作品を集めました。ほかには色鮮やかな葉鶏頭やダリア、そして胡桃や柘榴を様々に表現を加えています。竹内栖鳳《海幸》に描かれているのは、この時期から脂がのって美味しくなる鯖です。

18 霜降

ひと雨ごとに気温が下がり、霜も降り始めて、木々が色づいてくる季節。第五十四候「楓蔦黄（もみじつたきばむ）」にちなんで久保田米僊《蔦もみじ》を選びました。ほかには洛北八瀬や等持院の秋の風景を。また鹿とならんで鶉の鳴き声も秋の風情とされてきました。さらに秋の味覚松茸を描いた作品や、柿を象った作品も加えています。かつて大原女たちは、冬支度を前に、柴を頭にのせて街に売りに来ていました。

19 立冬

冬の始まりですが、巷では紅葉の盛りです。醍醐寺や栂尾の紅葉を描いた作品、錦眩い北大路魯山人《雲錦手大鉢》を選んでいます。第五十五候「山茶始開（つばきはじめてひらく）」は実は山茶花のこと。徳力富吉郎《初冬》にはまさにこの花が描かれています。これから旬を迎えるのが、蓮根や蕪といった根菜類。そして林檎を様々に解釈して表現した作品も加えました。

20 小雪

木々の葉が落ち、山間部で初雪が舞い始める頃、そのものの淋しさを竹内栖鳳《枯野の狐》は巧みに表現しています。これから鴛鴦の繁殖期、鮮やかなその姿は冬の景色に彩りを添えてくれます。冬の季語でもある兎や木兎を主題にした作品も選びました。葉の形が特徴的な石蕗はこの時期に可憐な黄色い花を咲かせ、紅葉が終わった木々は志村ふくみ《冬樹》のごとき姿となります。

21 大雪

本格的に冬が到来し、平野部でも初雪が見られます。織田一磨がリトグラフで描き留めたような雪の清水寺の風景は、現在ではなかなか見ることができませんが、ここでは雪にまつわる作品を集めました。鈴木治は、馬が雪の中にいることを、馬の身体に雪の結晶を描くことで表現しています。寒さが厳しくなるにつれ、ますます美味しさが増すのが蕪や大根など。それらを描いた作品も加えています。

22 冬至

陽が最も短いこの季節、厄払いや無病息災を祈る風習があります。かぼちゃ供養もその一つ。年末に向けて色々な市も賑わいます。富士に孔雀、獅子、仏手柑と多くの縁起物を集めたこの季節。極めつけは、初夢にちなんで、「事をなす」の《三茄子》です。

23 小寒

京都では一月十五日までが「松の内」。この日にお正月飾りを片づけ、鏡餅を開き、小豆粥を炊いて焼いたお餅を入れて食べます。鮒は、寒の入りのこの時期、脂がのって最も美味しくなります。第六十九候は「雉始雊（きじはじめてなく）」ですが、冬に羽毛を膨らませて福良雀と呼ばれるこの季節でとりあげました。そして麻田辨自《暮雪》に描かれた雉はまだつがいではありません。そんな中、わずかに春の息吹を伝えてくれる春蘭を主題にした作品を加えました。

24 大寒

寒さが最も厳しい季節。第七十一候「水沢腹堅（さわみずこおりつめる）」にちなみ氷や凍結を主題とした作品を集めました。この時期の花入れに、竹一重切を模した荒川豊蔵《黄瀬戸花入》を選んでいます。四代飯田新七による刺繍の《波濤図》は、その生地の色とも相まって、冬の海の荒々しさを想起させるものとしてここに加えています。

当館4階コレクション・ギャラリーで開催するコレクション展では、季節にちなんだテーマのみならず、ひとりの作家や芸術家グループの特集や、3階企画展会場で開催される展覧会の関連テーマなど、常に複数のテーマを構成しています。展示テーマが異なれば、同じ作品でも見方が変化し、それが持つ新たな意味の発見へと繋がります。「二十四節気」に沿って選ばれた本書の作品が、どのような別の表情を持っているのか、実際に美術館で是非探索してみてください。

［京都国立近代美術館学芸課長］

Life in Kyoto — Arts in Seasonal Delight: Works Illustrating the Twenty-four Seasonal Periods from the Collection of The National Museum of Modern Art, Kyoto

IKEDA Yuko

The National Museum of Modern Art, Kyoto and Its Collection

The National Museum of Modern Art, Kyoto is located within Okazaki Park, across the Kamo River on the eastern side from the center of Kyoto City. Facing the Museum is the Kyoto City KYOCERA Museum of Art, inaugurated in 1933 as Japan's second public art museum; and between these two museums rises the large *torii* gate, which is the entrance to Heian Jingu Shrine. In stark contrast to the Imperial Crown Style Kyoto City Museum of Art, which blends early twentieth-century Japanese and Western architectural styles, the Museum of Modern Art is a modern building composed of glass, steel, and granite. Designed by Maki Fumihiko, recipient of the Pritzker Prize, considered the Nobel Prize for architecture, this structure built in 1986 evokes the shoji paper panels and grid-shape of Kyoto's cityscape. On the fourth floor of the Museum building is a large window looking east, with a vista of the Eastern Hills, from Mt. Hiei in the north to Shogunzuka in the south, allowing visitors to view the landscape as the seasons change. The fourth floor also houses the Collection Gallery which offers exhibits from the Museum's collection.

The National Museum of Modern Art, Kyoto opened in its present site in 1963 as The Annex Museum of The National Museum of Modern Art in Tokyo, which was founded in 1952. The impetus for establishing a National Museum of Modern Art in Kyoto was the return of the Matsukata Collection by the French Government. However, as the French Government's condition for the return of the Matsukata Collection was that it be exhibited in Tokyo, the nation's capital, this did not materialize. In its stead, the establishment of the National Museum of Modern Art in Kyoto was conceived. As the capital of Japan for one thousand years from the Heian Period (794–1185), many people engaged in the arts have lived in Kyoto. Even after the transfer of the capital to Tokyo during the Meiji Restoration (1868), many of those artists remained in Kyoto to continue their creative activities, pursuing a new vision for the arts befitting the new era, and nurturing their successors. As an example, the Kyoto Prefectural School of Painting, founded before the Tokyo Fine Arts School, became the Kyoto City Technical School of Painting and the Kyoto City Technical School of Art, which merged as the Kyoto City University of Arts. The forerunners of Kyoto Institute of Technology incorporated engineering and design, and textile arts; classes in Japanese-style painting were offered by painters; Kansai Bijutsuin instructed students in Western-style painting and watercolors. In addition, the activities of studios and workshops of artisans have been important factors in modern Kyoto's artistic output. The artists who went out into the world from these institutions were actively involved in expositions and exhibitions from the latter nineteenth century into the twentieth century, playing a major role in the modernization of Japan's arts. Despite this, the main focus of Japan's history of modern art is presented as being Tokyo, the political center, and the role of Kyoto's artists has not gained sufficient recognition.

It was a matter of course that the new National Modern Art Museum located in Kyoto would have as one of its mandates the study of artists' activities since the Meiji Restoration centered around Kyoto and acquiring their artworks for its collection. As an art museum in Kyoto, a city with an "arts industry," the Museum's basic policy is one of active research and collection not only of works of fine arts in the form of paintings and sculptures, but also works in the field of applied arts, such as craftworks and design, which are more fully connected to the life of the people. These two principles continue to be the foundation for all of the Museum's programs.

In 1967, the National Museum of Modern Art Kyoto Annex became an independent entity as the National Museum of Modern Art, Kyoto. But the former Exhibition Hall for Industrial Affairs allocated by Kyoto City at the time of the Museum Annex's opening had no appropriate storage space nor did it have enough space to exhibit its permanent collection. It was only after the new Museum structure was built that more thorough collection, research, and exhibit activities based on the two foundational principles of the Museum could be achieved. In the thirty-four years since that time, the Museum has come to house some 12,700 works and materials. In the fourth-floor Collection Gallery, approximately 150 works are displayed in five themed rotations each year in Collection Exhibits.

Life in Kyoto — Arts in Seasonal Delight: Twenty-four seasonal periods seen in the collection

The major characteristic of The National Museum of Modern Art, Kyoto is the wide range of genres in its collection. They include Japanese-style paintings, oil paintings, watercolors, prints, sketches, sculptures, ceramics, lacquerware, metal ware, wood and bamboo ware, glass, textiles, figures, photographs; and other works that are cross-genre; as well as art materials that are indispensable to the understanding of artists' creative processes and artistic currents. The Museum collection also holds many works by foreign artists, their selection based on their association with Japan and its art.

In selecting works from the collection on the theme of "Life in Kyoto—Arts in Seasonal Delight" as related to twenty-four seasonal periods, efforts were made to encompass these various genres as much as possible. This means that works of the collection that do not fit within a particular season and many of the works by foreign artists that are among the major works of the collection (for example, Pablo Picasso's *Still Life – Palette, Candlestick and Head of a Minotaur*) are not included in this exhibit. This volume focuses on the "Twenty-four seasonal periods" showing the wide variety of the Museum's collection centered on Japanese-style paintings and craftworks traditionally closely connected to daily life rather than on the masterpieces in the collection.

The "Twenty-four seasonal periods" can further be divided into "Seventy-two seasonal stages." This volume has selected works with these two seasonal classifications in mind. However, due to the difference between the ancient calendar and current calendar and the climate warming of recent years, the seasonal effects do not always correspond to our actual concept of the seasons. A simple description of the works selected according to the seasonal periods is given below.

1 RISSHUN [Beginning of Spring]

This is the first of the twenty-four seasonal periods. Gathered here are works that feature camellias. In Morino Kako's Green Glaze Flower Vase, Red-Black Yōhen (Pyrofuzed) Style the red glaze extending over the green glaze likens it to a camellia. Spring Snow and Melting Snow are works that evoke the first of the seventy-two seasonal stages, "the east wind melts the ice." "Tsuchida Bakusen, who was from Sado Island in Niigata Prefecture, has written "painted in February" next to his seal in his painting Dish of Salmon, indicating that the fish is New Year's Aramaki salmon.

2 USU [Rain Water]

When snow turns to rain, the ume plum blossoms reach their peak. To complement pieces featuring plum blossoms, several works illustrate the sixth stage, "grasses and trees show signs of movement." Ikeda Yōson has painted the landscape near Byodo-in in Uji in "The Spring Breeze Opens the Door, Namu Amida Butsu," by Santoka. Kawabata Yanosuke has also featured the southern outskirts of Kyoto for his early spring landscape. Jyodai-bina Dolls and Folding Screen by Yoshida Hakurei and Fujii Tatsukichi is the sole set of bina dolls of the Doll Festival owned by the Museum.

3 KEICHITSU [Insects Awaken]

Befitting the time when spring gradually arrives and insects begin to move about, items featuring butterflies and lizards have been chosen. The flowers that bloom in this period are peach, tulip, Japanese quince, and magnolia. For his hanging scroll depicting a bird cage, a potted cymbidium, and other flowers, Nonagase Banka has given the title Long Spring Day, a seasonal word indicating that dusk seems to come later in the spring. To commemorate the Blue Dragon Festival held at Kiyomizu-dera Temple on March 14 and 15, works depicting the Goddess of Mercy and dragons have been selected.

4 SHUNBUN [Spring Equinox]

This day marks the start of longer days than nights. On the equinox, people pray at their ancestors' graves. A scene showing this rite is presented by Terashima Shimei's Prayer. After the spring equinox comes the cherry blossom season. Famed among the blossoms is the weeping cherry tree in Maruyama Park, a favorite subject of artists. However, Murakami Kagaku has chosen to set his Evening Scene of Cherry Blossoms Viewing at Hirano Shrine. A close look at the painting shows the word oden. From the food items placed on the folding platforms, it is clear that this term referred to grilled tofu with miso paste in those days. Another painting by Kagaku depicts a flatfish and a turban shell, seasonal foods in spring.

5 SEIMEI [Pure and Clear]

Spring is in full swing with everything looking clear and pure under the bright sunlight. While cherry blossoms are the main subjects, also included are works featuring flowers such as thistle and anemone. Gathered here are not only works showing the renowned cherry blossoms at Daigo-ji Temple, but also spring landscapes from around Kyoto, including Kitano, Awataguchi, and Kiyomizu-dera Temple. Of the many works by Sakamoto Hanjiro that feature horses, Horse with Foal has been selected as the breath of spring can be felt in this painting. Also shown is Nishimura Goun's Fresh Fish depicting sea bream, at its height in the spring season.

6 KOKU [Grain Rains]

Spring rains bless agricultural produce. The eighteenth seasonal stage is "peonies bloom." Seifu Yohei III and Kiyomizu Rokubei V have created works that demonstrate the results of their research into ancient ceramics using peonies as their subjects. With the rains, plants with vines in the bean family grow rapidly. Showing these plants are Kawai Unosuke's work of colored glaze of green leaves; Ikeda Taishin's lacquerware box using mother-of-pearl inlay; and expressing the deepening of the new green of bamboo grass is Kitamura Takeshi's kimono of tate-nishiki fabric, Bamboo Grass in Spring.

7 RIKKA [Beginning of Summer]

This is the season of the Boys' Day Festival. Tomita Keisen's Urashimako and Takase Kozani's Articulated Carp, which seems to move as if alive, are works associated with this time. And May is the time of the Hollyhock Festival (Aoi Matsuri), the subject of Ito Nisaburo's pair of woodblock prints, Aoi Festival. Ox-pulled court carriages from the Heian Period make an appearance in the procession. The featured plants in this period are hyacinth orchid, mustard, Japanese magnolia, and wisteria native to Japan. The twenty-first seasonal stage is "bamboo shoots sprout." The carved figurine of a bamboo shoot is shown with ume plums. For the tea ceremony, summer utensils are brought out along with a portable stove to heat water.

8 SHOMAN [Lesser Ripening]

When the trees and grasses are in full leaf, farmers prepare to plant rice seedlings. During this season of lovely fresh greenery, the Kifune Festival is held at Kifune Shrine, as are rites of court dances and music and parades of portable shrines. Lured by the mild weather, ladybugs and other insects as well as snails become active. Roses are what come to mind at this time. Imported after the Meiji Restoration (1868), these showy blooms of Western origin have held many people spellbound and have become subjects for artwork. This is also the time when wheat is harvested, called "wheat's autumn."

9   *BOSHU* [Grain Beards and Seeds]

In this season of planting grain seeds, the rainy season arrives. The flower that signifies the rainy season is hydrangea. Japanese meadowsweet, drawn on Kawai Unosuke's ceramic piece is a plant of the rose family native to Japan. Selected are pieces showing seasonal fruits: loquats, cherries, and tomatoes. Takase Kozan's *Mantis* reflects the twenty-fifth period "praying mantises hatch"; while Fukumoto Shitoko's *Summer Kimono Cloth: Light* evokes the glow of fireflies from the twenty-seventh period, "rotten grasses turn into fireflies."

10   *GESHI* [Summer Solstice]

This is the time of the longest daylight. The twenty-ninth period, "irises bloom," is illustrated by Yasuda Yukihiko's painting. Kiyomizu Rokubei IV's vase depicts a daylily with an art nouveau-style design. Citrus and dropwort flowers are also skillfully interwoven into the composition. Fukuda Heihachiro's *Swordfish* and several works in glass offer up a hint of coolness. As seen in Chigusa Soun's *Summer Shinto Ritual at Shimogamo-jinja Shrine*, in this season people step through a large loop made of reeds and pray to guard against illness and disasters.

11   *SHOSHO* [Lesser Heat]

In association with the Tanabata Star Festival on July 7 of the modern calendar, works portraying *The Tale of the Bamboo Cutter* are selected. When the end of the rainy season draws near and the heat becomes more intense, lotuses and water lilies bloom in gardens around Kyoto, as along the ditch by Higashi Hongan-ji Temple seen in Fudo Ritsuzan's *Shower*. Several varieties of expressions of these flowers are shown. Other plants include the silk tree; safflower, which appears in *The Tale of Genji*; and the summer vegetable cucumber. Hannah Höch's *Summer in Japan* was donated to commemorate her first solo exhibition in Japan at the Museum in 1974.

12   *TAISHO* [Greater Heat]

Isoda Mataichiro's *Summer Interior Scene* reveals several ways people seek some cooling from the heat of the summer within daily life. Outdoors, people find shade beneath trees and eat shaved ice to withstand the heat. Goldfish impart a cooling feeling and are a favorite of the season. For children this is the time of summer vacation, shown in works depicting the ocean and a beetle. A set of plates of Shishigadani pumpkins, with their unique shape, represents a vegetable in season. August 1 is Hassaku, when *geiko* and *maiko* entertainers in formal kimono call on their customers, instructors, and others to thank them for their support.

13   *RISSHU* [Beginning of Autumn]

Around the time when "Mid-summer heat greetings" give way to "Late-summer lingering heat greetings," the Tanabata Star Festival of the old calendar occurs. As the heat persists, the works chosen feature sunflowers, bamboo grass, and kudzu flowers. Common among works of this season are those that depict or are carved melon shapes. As seasonal foods, there are Yasui Sotaro's *Peaches* and Ando Ryokuzan's *Carved Ivory Figurine of Corn* which looks just like the real thing. Tanabe Chiku'unsai II's bamboo vase is literally *Beginning of Autumn*.

14   *SHOSHO* [Manageable Heat]

When the heat finally begins to subside, morning glories that have grown up to the eaves of houses are seen everywhere in the city. Morning glories, fringed pinks, and roses of Sharon are flowers that exude a cooling effect while giving off a hint of the vestiges of summer. Works with those features have been selected. The title of works by Fukuda Heihachiro and Fukami Toji—*Cool Morning*—refers to the freshness of the morning. The scene is imbued with airiness in the photograph by Nojima Yasuzo titled *Early Autumn*.

15   *HAKURO* [White Dew]

In this season when the morning dew falls on plants, Yamaguchi Kayo's *White Dew (Early Autumn)* has drawn the season itself in its subject matter of sunflowers. Of the many works in the Museum's collection, this is the only one whose title is the seasonal period itself. Ikeda Yoson has drawn spiderwort ("dew grass" in Japanese) in his *Dim Moonlight*. Other selections include some of the seven plants of autumn such as bush clover and balloon flower; and cockscomb and fiery red spider lily. Here is also master of modern paintings of beauties, Kaburaki Kiyokata on the subject of the Chrysanthemum Festival. As autumn approaches, snipes fly into Kyoto's districts.

16   *SHUBUN* [Autumn Equinox]

From the equinox, daytime becomes shorter. According to the forty-eighth seasonal stage, "farmers drain fields," this is the time to prepare for harvesting rice. The works chosen feature rice, autumn wind, and autumn fields as their subjects. The harvest moon that rises at this time is expertly captured in Kiyomizu Rokubei VI's *Jar with Waning Moon Design* and Kamisaka Yukichi's *Letter Box with Design: Hare in the Moon*. Autumn is also the setting for the ballad drama *Shinoda Zuma* (The Wife from Shinoda Forest) and the Noh drama *Izutsu* (The Well Cradle).

17   *KANRO* [Cold Dew]

When the cold dew falls, one of the three major unusual festivals of Kyoto, the Ox Festival, is held at Koryu-ji Temple to pray for abundant crops and to ward off the devil. The fiftieth seasonal stage is "chrysanthemums bloom." Illustrated are many different forms of chrysanthemums focusing on craftworks. Other works feature bright-colored amaranthus tricolor and dahlias, and walnuts and pomegranates. In *Mackerels and Prawns*, Takeuchi Seiho has drawn mackerels which are fatty and delicious this season.

18 SOKO [Frost Falls]

With each rainfall, the temperature turns colder, and frost starts to form, as trees become tinted with color. Kubota Beisen's *Icy Turning into Yellow and Red* embodies the fifty-fourth seasonal stage "maple leaves turn yellow." Other selections represent autumn landscapes of Yase and Toji-in Temple in northern Kyoto. Along with the cry of deer, the call of quail conveys the aura of autumn. Illustrated are works showing the tastes of autumn: mushrooms and carved persimmon. In days past, Oharame women peddlers came carrying firewood on their heads as people prepared for winter.

19 RITTO [Beginning of Winter]

The calendar indicates the beginning of winter, but the town is filled with colors of autumn foliage. Selected are works showing the fall colors of Daigo-ji Temple and Toganoo; and Kitaoji Rosanjin's *Large Bowl with Cherry Blossoms and Maple Trees Design* depicting the splendor of the fall colors. The fifty-fifth seasonal stage "first camellias bloom" actually refers to sasanqua. Tokuriki Tomikichiro's *Early Winter* is a treatment of sasanqua flowers. Lotus root and turnip are seasonal root vegetables. Also illustrated are works that represent apples in various ways.

20 SHOSETSU [Lesser Snow]

As the time approaches when the leaves fall from the trees and the first snow of the season dances in the mountains, Takeuchi Seiho's *Fox in Desolate Field* deftly captures winter's forlornness. In this breeding season for mandarin ducks, their bright appearance adds color to the winter landscape. Works chosen include those with the subjects of rabbits and horned owls, seasonal words for winter. With its characteristically-shaped leaves, the Japanese silver leaf presents charming yellow flowers; and trees that have lost their leaves appear as in *Pongee Kimono: Winter Tree* by Shimura Fukumi.

21 TAISETSU [Greater Snow]

With the advent of winter, snow falls on the plains. It is rare nowadays to see the snowy landscape of Kiyomizu-dera Temple, as depicted in Oda Kazuma's lithograph. Works relating to snow have been selected for this season. Suzuki Osamu has represented the horse as being in the snow by depicting snowflakes on the horse's body. The taste of turnips and daikon are enhanced in the depths of the cold. Works suggesting this have been included.

22 TOJI [Winter Solstice]

When the days are the shortest, people engage in customs to pray for warding off evil and for health and avoidance of disaster. One of these is the pumpkin purification rite. Many fairs are held as the year end approaches. "Bamboo and Swallows" designs are common, and birds plump up with feathers in this season. Then the New Year arrives. Symbols of good fortune are illustrated: Mt. Fuji, peacocks, *shishi* lions, Buddha's hands. The ultimate among these is the *Carved Ivory Figurine of Three Eggplants*, as the word for eggplant is a homonym for "to accomplish things," giving rise to the saying that it is good fortune to dream of eggplants as one's first dream of the New Year.

23 SHOKAN [Lesser Cold]

In Kyoto, the New Year period lasts until January 15. On this day, New Year's decorations are put away, the large rice cake is broken up, rice gruel with adzuki beans is cooked and eaten with toasted pieces of rice cake. At this time of winter chill, crucian carp are at the peak of flavor. The sixty-ninth seasonal stage is "pheasants start to call," but the pheasant in Asada Benji's *Snow in the Evening* has yet to find its mate. Complementing the winter cold is a piece with a spring orchid as its subject.

24 DAIKAN [Greater Cold]

This is the coldest time of year. Alluding to the seventy-first seasonal stage "ice thickens on streams," Illustrated are works with ice and freezing as their subject matter. The red berries of nandina provide color against the pale background. Arakawa Toyozo's *Yellow Seto Ware Flower Vase*, in the shape of a stalk of bamboo, is a fitting vase for this season. Iida Shinshichi IV's embroidery piece *Waves* recalls the roughness of the winter sea in the way the material and stitches match each other.

Multiple themes are curated for exhibits in the Collection Gallery on the Museum's fourth floor, not only relating to the seasons, but also in special showings of solo or group artists, or in association with the themed exhibits on the third floor. The same work can be viewed through a different perspective under another exhibition theme, and can lead to discovery of a new meaning. In the same way, visitors to the Museum can discover alternate expressions of the works chosen for this volume "Life in Kyoto—Arts in Seasonal Delight."

[Chief Curator, The National Museum of Modern Art, Kyoto]

あ

作家名 Artist	作品名 Title	制作年 Date	材質 Medium	技法 Technique	形状 Form	寸法 (cm: 高×幅×奥行) Size (cm: h × w × d)	節気 Seasonal Period	掲載頁 page of illustration
赤塚自得 AKATSUKA Jitoku	香合 桜花鍍縁 Incense Container with Cherry Blossoms Design with Tin Brim	大正時代 1912-26	木胎、漆、金、錫 wood, lacquer, gold, tin	高蒔絵 taka maki-e		3.5 × 7.0 × 9.0	春分 | SHUNBUN Spring Equinox	33
秋野不矩 AKINO Fuku	残雪 Melting Snow	昭和55 1980	紙本 color on paper	着色	額 framed	149.0 × 271.0	立春 | RISSHUN Beginning of Spring	8
浅井忠 ASAI Chu	薔薇図 Roses	明治35-40 1902-07	紙本 color on paper	着色	軸 hanging scroll	30.0 × 54.0	小満 | SHOMAN Lesser Ripening	66
麻田辨自 ASADA Benji	曲水 Carving Stream	昭和44 1969	紙本 color on paper	着色	二曲一隻屏風 two-panels folding screen	169.0 × 185.0	小雪 | SHOSETSU Lesser Snow	169
麻田辨自 ASADA Benji	宵雪 Snow in the Evening	昭和55 1980	紙本 color on paper	着色	額 framed	161.0 × 130.0	小寒 | SHOKAN Lesser Cold	190
旭玉山 ASAHI Gyokuzan	葛に蜘蛛の巣図文庫 Letter Box with Kudzu Vine and Spider Web Design	明治43 1910	木、鉛、貝 wood, lead, shell	螺鈿 raden inlay		12.0 × 28.0 × 37.5	立秋 | RISSHU Beginning of Autumn	111
足立源一郎 ADACHI Gen'ichiro	チューリップ Tulips	大正6/9 1917/20	画布 oil on canvas	油彩	額 framed	45.5 × 53.0	啓蟄 | KEICHITSU Insects Awaken	27
新井謹也 ARAI Kin'ya	等持院秋庭 Autumn Garden of Tōji-in Temple	明治43 1910	板 oil on board	油彩	額 framed	25.5 × 30.0	霜降 | SOKO Frost Falls	151
浅野竹二 ASANO Takeji	金魚屋 Goldfish Vendor	昭和28 1953	紙 paper	木版 woodblock print		33.0 × 22.7	大暑 | TAISHO Greater Heat	99
荒川豊蔵 ARAKAWA Toyozo	黄瀬戸花入 Yellow Seto Ware Flower Vase	昭和42 1967	陶器、釉薬 ceramic, glaze		一口	27.0 × 12.0 × 12.0	大寒 | DAIKAN Greater Cold	196
安藤十兵衛 ANDO Jubei	薬艶頭図花瓶 Flower Vases with Amaranthus Tricolor	明治~大正時代 1868-1926	金属、釉薬 metal glaze	有線七宝 wired cloisonné	一対 pair of vases	44.5 × 18.0 × 18.0 (各: each)	寒露 | KANRO Cold Dew	143
安藤十兵衛 ANDO Jubei	竹に雀図七宝花瓶 Cloisonne Flower Vases with Bamboo and Sparrow Design	明治~大正時代 1868-1926	金属、釉薬 metal glaze	有線七宝 wired cloisonné	一対 pair of vases	25.2 × 10.5 × 10.5 (各: each)	冬至 | TOJI Winter Solstice	184
安藤緑山 ANDO Ryokuzan	貝尽くし 牙彫置物 Carved Ivory Figurines of Shellfish	大正~昭和初 c. 1912-30	象牙 ivory	彫刻、着色 carved, dyed		[ツノガイ: horned tusk] 6.0 × 10.0 × 9.0 [トコブシ: tokobushi] 2.0 × 6.0 × 5.0 [蛤: hard clam] 2.0 × 4.0 × 5.0	春分 | SHUNBUN Spring Equinox	32
安藤緑山 ANDO Ryokuzan	竹の子に梅 牙彫置物 Carved Ivory Figurine of a Bamboo Shoot with Plums	大正~昭和初 c. 1912-30	象牙 ivory	彫刻、着色 carved, dyed		25.9 × 18.0 × 37.0	立夏 | RIKKA Beginning of Summer	60

作家名 Artist	作品名 Title	制作年 Date	材質 Medium	技法 Technique	形状 Form	寸法（cm：高×幅×奥行） Size (cm; h × w × d)	節気 Seasonal Period	掲載頁 page of illustration
石川光明 ISHIKAWA Komei	蓮根に蛙 牙彫置物 Carved Ivory Figurine of Lotus Root with Frog	明治時代 1868-1912	象牙 ivory	彫刻、染色 carved, dyed		8.0 × 31.3 × 12.7	立冬｜RITTO Beginning of Winter	165
石黒宗麿 ISHIGURO Munemaro	柿釉金彩鉢 Bowl, Reddish-brown Glaze with Gold Paint	昭和43 1968	陶器、釉薬 ceramic, glaze	金彩 gold paint		8.5 × 35.0 × 35.0	霜降｜SOKO Frost Falls	155
伊島薫 IJIMA Kaoru	無題—1（ひまわりの花） Untitled-1 (Sunflower)	昭和64 1989	紙 paper	ポラロイド（20 × 24） polaroid (20 × 24)		61.0 × 51.0	立秋｜RISSHU Beginning of Autumn	108
磯田又一郎 ISODA Mataichiro	夏座敷 Summer Interior Scene	昭和11 1936	紙本 color on paper	着色	二曲一隻屏風 two-panels folding screen	184.5 × 221.0	大暑｜TAISHO Greater Heat	101
伊谷賢蔵 ITANI Kenzo	南瓜などの静物 Pumpkin and Other Still Life	昭和34 1959	画布 oil on canvas	油彩	額 framed	116.5 × 80.4	白露｜HAKURO White Dew	130
板谷波山 ITAYA Hazan	朝陽磁鶴首花瓶 Flower Vase with Crane's Neck Shape Design, Copper Glaze	昭和13 1938	磁器、釉薬 porcelain, glaze			31.0 × 13.8 × 13.8	正月｜BOSHU The New Year	202
伊藤久三郎 ITO Kyuzaburo	雨戒いは感傷 Rainfall or Sentiment	昭和12 1937	画布 oil on canvas	油彩	額 framed	112.5 × 145.5	小満｜SHOMAN Lesser Ripening	64
伊藤草白 ITO Sohaku	枇杷 Loquats	c.1930 昭和5頃	紙本 color on paper	着色	額 framed	208.6 × 105.4	芒種｜BOSHU Grain Beards and Seeds	76
伊藤草白 ITO Sohaku	松茸図 Matsu-take Mushrooms	昭和初期 c.1926-40	紙本 color on paper	着色	軸 hanging scroll	36.5 × 43.6	霜降｜SOKO Frost Falls	154
三代伊東陶山 ITO Tozan III	秋映花器 Flower Vase: Autumn Glow	1966 昭和41	陶器、釉薬 ceramic, glaze			39.0 × 17.0 × 17.0	秋分｜SHUBUN Autumn Equinox	132
伊藤仁三郎 ITO Nisaburo	二条院春雪 Spring Snow in Nison-in Temple	昭和35-44 1960-69	紙 paper	木版 woodblock print		40.5 × 27.2	立春｜RISSHUN Beginning of Spring	10
伊藤仁三郎 ITO Nisaburo	嵐山春景 Spring Scene in Arashiyama	昭和35-44 1960-69	紙 paper	木版 woodblock print		15.8 × 23.3	春分｜SHUNBUN Spring Equinox	38
伊藤仁三郎 ITO Nisaburo	葵祭り① Aoi Festival 1	昭和35-44 1960-69	紙 paper	木版 woodblock print		27.2 × 40.2	立夏｜RIKKA Beginning of Summer	57
伊藤仁三郎 ITO Nisaburo	葵祭り② Aoi Festival 2	昭和35-44 1960-69	紙 paper	木版 woodblock print		27.0 × 40.5	立夏｜RIKKA Beginning of Summer	57
伊藤仁三郎 ITO Nisaburo	雪の鞍馬 Snow in Kurama	昭和35-44 1960-69	紙 paper	木版 woodblock print		27.1 × 24.0	大寒｜DAIKAN Greater Cold	195

作品リスト | List of Works

作家名 Artist	作品名 Title	制作年 Date	材質 Medium	技法 Technique	形状 Form	寸法 (cm:高×幅×奥行) Size (cm: h × w × d)	節気 Seasonal Period	掲載頁 page of illustration
植松包美 UEMATSU Hobi	梅蒔絵硯箱 Inkstone Box with Plum Blossom Design, Maki-e	大正時代 1912-26	木胎、漆、金 wood, lacquer, gold	蒔絵 maki-e		5.3 × 21.0 × 24.8	雨水 | USUI Rainwater	16
上村松園 UEMURA Shoen	虹を見る Looking up at the Rainbow	昭和7 1932	絹本 color on silk	着色	三曲一双屏風 (各：each) pair of two-panels folding screens	182.0 × 181.0 (各：each)	白露 | HAKURO White Dew	125
牛島憲之 USHIJIMA Noriyuki	晩春 Late Spring	昭和29 1954	画布 oil on canvas	油彩	framed	64.5 × 90.5	穀雨 | KOKU Grain Rains	53
宇田荻邨 UDA Tekison	水神貴船奥宮 Inmost Shrine of Kifune Enshrining the God of Water	昭和44 1969	紙本 color on paper	着色	framed	98.0 × 82.5	小満 | SHOMAN Lesser Ripening	65
梅原龍三郎 UMEHARA Ryuzaburo	洛北八瀬の秋 Autumn in Yase, the Northern Suburbs of Kyoto	明治40 1907	板 oil on board	油彩	額 framed	23.5 × 33.0	霜降 | SOKO Frost Falls	151
海野勝珉 UNNO Shomin	椿小禽図花瓶 Vase with Birds and Camellias Design	明治時代 1868-1912	銀 silver	象嵌（金、赤銅、四分一） inlay (gold, shakudo, shibuichi copper alloy)		29.0 × 17.0 × 17.0	立春 | RISSHUN Beginning of Spring	11
遠藤享 ENDO Susumu	Space & Space (Apple IV) Space & Space (Apple IV)	昭和60 1985	紙 paper	オフセット、リトグラフ offset, lithograph		45.0 × 45.0	立夏 | RIKKA Beginning of Summer	164
大下春香 OSHITA Sekko	朴の花文庫 Covered Letter Box with Magnolia Design	昭和10 1935	木胎、漆、金 wood, lacquer, gold	蒔絵 maki-e		22.2 × 24.4 × 29.4	大暑 | TAISHO Greater Heat	61
大須賀喬 OSUGA Takashi	昆虫文小匣 Casket with Insects Design	昭和22 1947	洋銀 nickel silver	鍛造、彫金 wrought, carved		8.0 × 9.0 × 17.2	小満 | SHOMAN Lesser Ripening	68
大須賀喬 OSUGA Takashi	仙人掌文香盒 Incense Tray with Cacatus Design	昭和11 1936	赤銅 red copper	鍛造、彫金 wrought, carved		3.2 × 34.7 × 34.7	小暑 | SHOSHO Lesser Heat	95
太田喜二郎 OTA Kijiro	洛北の農家 A Farmhouse of Rakuhoku (Northern Area of Kyoto)	大正13 1924	画布 oil on canvas	油彩	額 framed	130.0 × 145.0	大暑 | TAISHO Greater Heat	100
大西茂 ONISHI Shigeru	凍結 Frozen	昭和30 1955		多重露光、フォトグラム multiple exposure, photogram		28.1 × 36.0	大寒 | DAIKAN Greater Cold	199
大西茂 ONISHI Shigeru	冬鏡 Winter Mirror	昭和30 1955		多重露光、フォトグラム multiple exposure, photogram		24.7 × 31.1	大寒 | DAIKAN Greater Cold	199
岡田章人 OKADA Akihito	彫漆木瓜之図匣 Box with Japanese Quince Design, Choshitsu Technique	昭和38 1963	木、漆 wood, lacquer	彫漆 carved lacquer		15.2 × 17.7 × 30.4	啓蟄 | KEICHITSU Insects Awaken	29

作家名 Artist	作品名 Title	制作年 Date	材質 Medium	技法 Technique	形状 Form	寸法 (cm：高×幅×奥行) Size (cm: h × w × d)	節気 Seasonal Period	掲載頁 page of illustration
加藤宗巌 KATO Sogan	しの田の森の秋宵 Autumn Evening in Shinoda Forest (Scene from the Folklore "Shinoda-zuma")	昭和56 1981	銅 copper	鍍銀、金彩 silver impregnation, gold paint		47.0 × 21.0 × 18.0	秋分｜SHUBUN Autumn Equinox	137
加藤土師萌 KATO Hajime	黄地紅彩麗雲文角皿 Square Dish with Dragon and Cloud Design, Yellow Glaze and Overglaze Red	昭和28 1953	磁器、釉薬 porcelain, glaze			3.5 × 18.5 × 18.5	啓蟄｜KEICHITSU Insects Awaken	28
加藤土師萌 KATO Hajime	齊柚紅彩菊文鉢 Bowl with Horned Owl Design, Cobalt Glaze, Overglaze Enamels with Misty Patterns	昭和36 1961	陶器、釉薬 ceramic, glaze			11.0 × 30.5 × 30.5	寒露｜KANRO Cold Dew	143
加藤土師萌 KATO Hajime	吹墨色絵菊花文飾壺 Ornamental Jar with Chrysanthemum Design, Overglaze Enamels with Misty Glaze	c.1968	陶器、釉薬 ceramic, glaze	色絵 overglaze enamels		20.0 × 19.4 × 19.4	小雪｜SHOSETSU Lesser Snow	169
金田和郎 KANADA Waro	雨中牡丹図 Peonies in the Rain	大正9頃 c.1920	絹本 color on silk	着色	軸 hanging scroll	134.0 × 42.0	穀雨｜KOKU Grain Rains	50
香取秀眞 KATORI Hozuma	みみずく香炉 Horned Owl-shaped Incense Burner	昭和28 1953	青銅 bronze	鋳造、象嵌(金) casting, inlay (gold)		13.5 × 9.5 × 9.5	小雪｜SHOSETSU Lesser Snow	169
香取秀眞 KATORI Hozuma	木菟香炉 Horned Owl-shaped Incense Burner	昭和23 1948	青銅 bronze	鋳造 casting		11.0 × 6.0 × 7.0	小雪｜SHOSETSU Lesser Snow	169
叶 光夫 KANO Mitsuo	天藍釉壺「流」 Vase with Indigo Cobalt Glaze: Flowing	昭和39 1964	磁器、釉薬 porcelain glaze			36.5 × 38.0 × 38.0	夏至｜GESHI Summer Solstice	83
鏑木清方 KABURAKI Kiyokata	菊花節 The Chrysanthemum Festival	昭和17 1942	絹本 color on silk	着色	軸 hanging scroll	130.0 × 58.0	白露｜HAKURO White Dew	126
鎌倉芳太郎 KAMAKURA Yoshitaro	紅型上布竹文夏長着 Summer Kimono with Bamboo Design	昭和43 1968	芭蕉布 banana-leaf cloth	紅型染 Bingata stencil dyed		168.0 × 66.0 (着丈: sleeve length)	大暑｜TAISHO Greater Heat	103
神坂松濤 KAMISAKA Shoto	椿 Camellias	明治末 c.1900-12	絹本 color on silk	着色	額 framed	118.5 × 86.0	立春｜RISSHUN Beginning of Spring	12
神坂松濤 KAMISAKA Shoto	白川女 Shirakawame (Woman from Shirakawa Selling Flowers)	明治末 c.1900-12	木本 color on silk	着色	軸 hanging scroll	116.4 × 50.1	秋分｜SHUBUN Autumn Equinox	136
神坂雪佳(案)／ 神坂祐吉(作) KAMISAKA Sekka (design) / KAMISAKA Yukichi (lacquerware)	石畳図蝶鈿時絵煙草箱 Cigarette Box with Japanese Silver Leaf Design, Maki-e and Raden Inlay	明治末～大正初 c.1910-20	木、漆、金、貝 wood, lacquer, gold, shell	蒔絵、螺鈿 maki-e, raden inlay		5.2 × 14.0 × 11.5	小雪｜SHOSETSU Lesser Snow	166
神坂祐吉 KAMISAKA Yukichi	月象之図 硯付手箱 Letter Box with Design: Hare in the Moon	[不詳] [n.d.]	木、漆、貝 wood, lacquer, shell	螺鈿 raden inlay		18.8 × 22.7 × 37.7	秋分｜SHUBUN Autumn Equinox	137

作品リスト｜List of Works

作家名 Artist	作品名 Title	制作年 Date	材質 Medium	技法 Technique	形状 Form	寸法(cm：高×幅×奥行) Size (cm: h × w × d)	節気 Seasonal Period	掲載頁 page of illustration
河合卯之助 KAWAI Unosuke	京鹿の子画瓶 Bottle with Japanese Meadowsweet Design	昭和15 1940	陶器、釉薬 ceramic, glaze	色絵 overglaze enamels		22.2 × 26.0 × 26.0	芒種 BOSHU Grain Beards and Seeds	74
河合卯之助 KAWAI Unosuke	蚕豆蠅蟇彩画合子 Small Covered Box with Young Broad-bean Leaf, Overglaze Enamels	[不詳] [n.d.]	陶器、釉薬 ceramic, glaze	色絵 overglaze enamels		8.6 × 11.5 × 11.5	穀雨 KOKU Grain Rains	51
河合卯之助 KAWAI Unosuke	呉須赤絵南天木指 Water Container with Nandina Design, Blue and Red Overglaze Enamels	[不詳] [n.d.]	陶器、釉薬 ceramic, glaze			14.8 × 13.7 × 13.7	大寒 DAIKAN Greater Cold	196
河井寛次郎 KAWAI Kanjiro	鉄薬丸紋鉢(丸紋筮絵鉢) Iron Glazed Bowl with Circle Pattern Design	昭和16 1941	陶器、釉薬 ceramic, glaze	轆轤成形 wheel making		8.0 × 27.0 × 27.0	立秋 RISSHU Beginning of Autumn	112
河津光峻 KAWAZU Koshun	梅咲く早春 Early Spring in Plum Orchard	昭和10年代 1935-45	紙本 color on paper	着色 color on paper	額 framed	103.7 × 145.0	雨水 USUI Rainwater	15
川西英 KAWANISHI Hide	得尾紅葉 Red Leaves in Toganoo	昭和14 1939	紙 paper	木版 woodblock print		59.0 × 45.2	立冬 RITTO Beginning of Winter	160
川西英 KAWANISHI Hide	雨後庭園(佳麗宮) The Garden after Raining, Katsura Detached Palace	昭和30 1955	紙 paper	木版 woodblock print		32.4 × 48.0	小満 SHOMAN Lesser Ripening	67
川端弥之助 KAWABATA Yanosuke	坂南早春 Early Spring in the South Suburb of Kyoto	昭和14 1939	画布 oil on canvas	油彩	額 framed	47.1 × 82.0	雨水 USUI Rainwater	20
川端龍子 KAWABATA Ryushi	佳人好任 Summer Parlor	大正14 1925	絹本 color on silk	着色	額 framed	136.3 × 115.1	夏至 GESHI Summer Solstice	81
河村蒹太郎 KAWAMURA Kitaro	色絵牡丹蝶之図喰籠 Covered Box with Butterfly and Peony Design, Overglaze Enamels	昭和初期 c.1926-40	磁器、釉薬 porcelain, glaze	染付、色絵 blue underglaze, overglaze enamels		15.0 × 27.0 × 27.0	穀雨 KOKU Grain Rains	50
川原林秀国 KAWARABAYASHI Hidekuni	瓜形香炉 Oriental-Melon-shaped Incense Burner	明治23 1890	銀 silver	平象嵌(金、素銅) inlay (gold, copper)		10.0 × 12.0 × 9.5	立秋 RISSHU Beginning of Autumn	111
菊池契月 KIKUCHI Keigetsu	桜 Cherry Blossoms	昭和4 1929	紙本 paper	墨画淡彩 sumi ink and tint color on paper	軸 hanging scroll	171.0 × 94.5	春分 SHUNBUN Spring Equinox	39
輝山 Kizan	花蝶尽し鉢 Bowl with Plethora of Flowers and Butterflies Design	明治～大正時代 1868-1926	陶器、釉薬 ceramic, glaze	色絵、盆彩 overglaze enamels, gold paint		5.1 × 12.2 × 12.2	清明 SEIMEI Pure and Clear	43
岸田劉生 KISHIDA Ryusei	童女と菊花 Young Girl and Chrysanthemums	大正9 1920	紙 paper	木版 woodblock print		32.7 × 48.4	寒露 KANRO Cold Dew	148
北大路魯山人 KITAOJI Rosanjin	染付花鳥花入 Flower Vase with Flower and Bird Design, Blue Underglaze	昭和14頃 c.1939	磁器、釉薬 porcelain, glaze	染付 blue underglaze		29.5 × 21.0 × 21.0	冬至 TOJI Winter Solstice	183

作家名 Artist	作品名 Title	制作年 Date	材質 Medium	技法 Technique	形状 Form	寸法 (cm: 高 h × 幅 w × 奥行 d) Size	節気 Seasonal Period	掲載頁 page of illustration
北大路魯山人 KITAOJI Rosanjin	糸目菊絵桶 Covered Bowl with Chrysanthemum Design	昭和19頃 c.1944	木胎, 漆 wood, lacquer			10.6 × 16.9 × 16.9 (各: each)	寒露 KANRO Cold Dew	146
北大路魯山人 KITAOJI Rosanjin	色絵金彩椿文鉢 Bowl with Camellia Design, Overglaze Enamels and Gold	昭和30 1955	陶器, 釉薬 ceramic, glaze	色絵, 金彩 overglaze enamels, gold paint		20.0 × 36.0 × 36.0	立春 RISSHUN Beginning of Spring	13
北大路魯山人 KITAOJI Rosanjin	雲錦手大鉢 Large Bowl with Cherry-blossoms and Maple Trees Design	昭和33 1958	陶器, 釉薬 ceramic, glaze	金彩 gold paint		17.2 × 33.0 × 33.0	立冬 RITTO Beginning of Winter	162
北沢映月 KITAZAWA Eigetsu	祇園会 Gion Festival	昭和11 1936	絹本 color on silk	着色 color	二曲一隻屏風 two-panels folding screen	177.0 × 226.0	小暑 SHOSHO Lesser Heat	90
北村武資 KITAMURA Takeshi	経錦着物「笹の春」 Kimono of 'Tate-nishiki Fabric: Bamboo Grass in Spring'	平成23 2011	絹 silk	経錦 tate-nishiki weaving		189.0 × 138.0	穀雨 KOKU(U) Grain Rains	49
北村武資 KITAMURA Takeshi	タペストリー[脚々] Tapestry: Spring Growing Grass	昭和53 1978	絹 silk	変織 unique weaving		168.0 × 91.0	雨水 USUI Rainwater	21
北原千鹿 KITAHARA Senroku	鶴文金彩壺 Jar with Quail Design in Gold	昭和13 1938	黄銅 brass	鍛造, 彫金 wrought, carved		19.0 × 24.5 × 24.5	霜降 SOKO Frost Falls	156
北村今三 KITAMURA Imazo	金魚 Goldfish	c.1932 昭和7頃	紙 paper	木版, 着色 woodblock print, hand colored		14.3 × 14.2	大暑 TAISHO Greater Heat	99
北脇昇 KITAWAKI Noboru	秋の驚異 Wonder in Autumn	c.1945 昭和20頃	油布 oil on canvas		額 framed	33.5 × 45.5	雨水 USUI Rainwater	150
木村盛伸 KIMURA Morinobu	釣窯 大鉢 Large Bowl, Jun Ware Style	昭和58 1983	陶器, 釉薬 ceramic, glaze			16.0 × 32.5 × 32.5	春分 SHUNBUN Spring Equinox	34
木村雨山 KIMURA Uzan	友禅着物 Kimono, Yuzen Dyed	昭和40年代 1965-75	絹 silk	友禅 yuzen dyed		168.0 × 134.0	小寒 SHOKAN Lesser Cold	192
木村雨山 KIMURA Uzan	変織縮緬訪問着「花」 Silk Crepe Kimono, Flower	昭和40 1965	縮緬 silk crepe	友禅 yuzen dyed		163.0 × 64.0 (裄丈: sleeve length)	啓蟄 KEICHITSU Insects Awaken	29
四代 清水六兵衛 KIYOMIZU Rokubei IV	荒磁模様蝶貝花瓶 Vase with Daylily Design, Raden Inlay	明治後期 c.1890-1912	磁器, 釉薬 ceramic, glaze	螺鈿 raden inlay		36.0 × 24.0 × 24.0	夏至 GESHI Summer Solstice	80
五代 清水六兵衛 KIYOMIZU Rokubei V	青華蘭四方花瓶 Square Vase with Orchid Design, Blue Underglaze	大正13 1924	磁器, 釉薬 porcelain, glaze	染付 blue underglaze		50.7 × 20.0 × 20.0	立夏 RIKKA Beginning of Summer	62
五代 清水六兵衛 KIYOMIZU Rokubei V	青羽陸牡丹唐草花瓶 Flower Vase with Peony in Scroll Style, Otozu Ware	昭和2 1927	陶器, 釉薬 ceramic, glaze			32.0 × 13.6 × 13.6	穀雨 KOKU(U) Grain Rains	51

く

作家名 / Artist	作品名 / Title	制作年 / Date	材質 / Medium	技法 / Technique	形状 / Form	寸法(cm, 高×幅×奥行) / Size (cm, h × w × d)	節気 / Seasonal Period	掲載頁 / page of illustration
五代 清水六兵衛 / KIYOMIZU Rokubei V	色絵秋草手鉢 / *Covered Brazier with Autumn Wild Flowers Design, Overglaze Enamels*	昭和15 / 1940	陶器、釉薬 / ceramic, glaze	色絵 / overglaze enamels		17.4 × 20.5 × 20.5	白露 | *HAKURO* / White Dew	127
六代 清水六兵衛 / KIYOMIZU Rokubei VI	睡蓮置物 / *Water Lily Ornament*	昭和9 / 1934	陶器、釉薬 / ceramic, glaze			【花:flower】 4.6 × 13.7 × 13.7 【帯:band】 5.0 × 4.7 × 4.7 【葉:leaf】 【大:large】 23.0 × 23.0 【中:middle】 15.0 × 15.0 【小:small】 14.0 × 14.0	小暑 | *SHOSHO* / Lesser Heat	92
六代 清水六兵衛 / KIYOMIZU Rokubei VI	紫陽花花瓶 / *Flower Vase with Hydrangea Design*	昭和16 / 1941	陶器、釉薬 / ceramic, glaze			37.2 × 28.0 × 25.6	芒種 | *BOSHU* / Grain Beards and Seeds	74
六代 清水六兵衛 / KIYOMIZU Rokubei VI	三彩向日葵飾皿 / *Ornamental Dish with Sun Flowers Design, Tri-colored Enameled Glaze*	昭和29 / 1954	陶器、釉薬 / ceramic, glaze			9.0 × 62.8 × 62.8	立秋 | *RISSHU* / Beginning of Autumn	108
六代 清水六兵衛 / KIYOMIZU Rokubei VI	古稀彩佐月壷 / *Jar with Waning Moon Design*	昭和48 / 1973	陶器、釉薬 / ceramic, glaze			30.0 × 38.0 × 38.0	秋分 | *SHUBUN* / Autumn Equinox	133
錦雲軒稲葉 / Kin'unken Inaba	花鳥図香炉 / *Incense Burner with Birds and Flowers Design*	明治〜大正時代 / 1868-1926	金属、釉薬 / metal, glaze	有線七宝 / wired cloisonné		32.5 × 27.0 × 27.0	立夏 | *RIKKA* / Beginning of Summer	58
七代 錦光山宗兵衛 / KINKOZAN Sobei VII	花蝶図大鉢 / *Large Bowl with Flowers and Butterflies Design*	明治〜大正時代 / 1868-1926	陶器、釉薬 / ceramic, glaze	色絵、金彩 / overglaze enamels, gold paint		10.9 × 27.6 × 27.6	清明 | *SEIMEI* / Pure and Clear	43
楠部彌弌 / KUSUBE Yaichi	彩埏春花瓶 / *Flower Vase with Mulan Magnolia Design in Spring Saien Technique*	昭和55 / 1980	磁器、釉薬 / porcelain, glaze			28.0 × 25.0 × 25.0	啓蟄 | *KEICHITSU* / Insects Awaken	25
楠部彌弌 / KUSUBE Yaichi	色絵梅花文花瓶 / *Vase with Plum Blossoms Design, Overglaze Enamels*	昭和12 / 1937	磁器、釉薬 / porcelain, glaze	色絵 / overglaze enamels		33.0 × 35.5 × 35.5	雨水 | *USUI* / Rainwater	16
楠部彌弌 / KUSUBE Yaichi	葡萄文花瓶 / *Flower Vase with Grapevine Design*	昭和2 / 1927	陶器、釉薬 / ceramic, glaze			36.0 × 28.0 × 28.0	処暑 | *SHOSHO* / Manageable Heat	117
国枝金三 / KUNIEDA Kinzo	粟田口より四月の夕 / *View from Awataguchi: Evening in April*	[不詳] / [n.d.]	紙 / paper	水彩 / watercolor	額 / framed	33.0 × 24.2	清明 | *SEIMEI* / Pure and Clear	45
国絵桂渓 / KUNIMATSU Keikei	茶店 / *Teahouse*	明治40 / 1907	紙 / paper	水彩 / watercolor	額 / framed	24.7 × 32.2	春分 | *SHUNBUN* / Spring Equinox	38
久保田米僊 / KUBOTA Beisen	蔦もみぢ / *Ivy Turning into Yellow and Red*	明治18 / 1885	絹本 / color on silk	着色 / color on silk	軸 / hanging scroll	123.7 × 46.8	霜降 | *SOKO* / Frost Falls	149
久保田米僊 / KUBOTA Beisen	水中落花蝶図 / *Floating Flowers and Butterflies*	明治中期 / 1875-95	絹本 / color on silk	着色 / color on silk	軸 / hanging scroll	126.0 × 51.0	啓蟄 | *KEICHITSU* / Insects Awaken	24

作家名 Artist	作品名 Title	制作年 Date	材質 Medium	技法 Technique	形状 Form	寸法（cm：高×幅×奥行） Size (cm: h × w × d)	節気 Seasonal Period	掲載頁 page of illustration
熊谷守一 KUMAGAI Morikazu	獅子頭 Head of Shishi (A Mask for Dance Dedicated to Gods)	昭和49 1974	板	油彩 oil on board	額 framed	24.0 × 33.0	正月 The New Year	203
黒田辰秋 KURODA Tatsuaki	蝋鈿瓜形茶器 Raden Inlaid Melon-shaped Tea Caddy	昭和24 1949	木、漆、貝 wood, lacquer, shell	蝋鈿 raden inlay		7.5 × 6.4 × 6.4	立秋 RISSHU Beginning of Autumn	111
黒田辰秋 KURODA Tatsuaki	乾漆梅花盆 Plum Blossom Shaped Tray, Dry Lacquer	昭和41 1966	木、漆 wood, lacquer	乾漆 dry lacquer		3.0 × 26.7 × 26.7	雨水 USUI Rainwater	18
黒田鵬 KURODA Toru	春宵 Spring Evening	昭和48 1973	布 cloth	型染 stencil dyed	二曲一隻屏風 two-panels folding screen	172.0 × 172.0	春分 SHUNBUN Spring Equinox	34
黒田鵬 KURODA Toru	雫降る夜 Sleeting Night	昭和51 1976	布 cloth	型染 stencil dyed	二曲一双屏風 pair of two-panels folding screens	48.5 × 31.0	啓蟄 KEICHITSU Insects Awaken	30
黒田重太郎 KURODA Jutaro	白川村 Shirakawa Village	明治38 1905	紙 paper	水彩 watercolor	額 framed	45.0 × 53.0	霜降 SOKO Frost Falls	157
ケヴィン・マルティーニ=フューラー Kevin MARTINI-FULLER	水蓮の池 Lilly Pond	昭和57 1982		ゼラチン・シルバー・プリント gelatin silver print		14.0 × 21.5	小暑 SHOSHO Lesser Heat	93
迎田秋悦 KODA Shuetsu	御所車蒔絵引戸 A Pair of Sliding Doors with Court Carriage Design, Maki-e	明治後期～昭和初 c.1900–30	木、漆 wood, lacquer	蒔絵 maki-e	引戸（二面）（各：each） pair of sliding doors	62.0 × 96.0 × 2.0 （各：each）	立夏 RIKKA Beginning of Summer	57
迎田秋悦 KODA Shuetsu	稲穂蒔絵六角香合 Hexagonal Incense Case of Rice Ears Design, Maki-e	昭和3 1928	木、漆、金 wood, lacquer, gold	蒔絵 maki-e		3.3 × 9.0 × 9.0	秋分 SHUBUN Autumn Equinox	134
呉藤友乗 GOTO Yujo	朱菊盤 Red Chrysanthemum-shaped Tray	昭和38 1963	木胎、漆 wood, lacquer			6.0 × 35.5 × 35.5	寒露 KANRO Cold Dew	148
小林清親 KOBAYASHI Kiyochika	柘榴に葡萄 Pomegranates and Grapes	[不詳] [n.d.]	紙 paper	木版 woodblock print		24.4 × 37.5	寒露 KANRO Cold Dew	145
小林古径 KOBAYASHI Kokei	竹取物語 The Tale of the Bamboo Cutter	大正6 1917	紙本	着色 color on paper	巻子 hand scroll	45.0 × 659.5	小暑 SHOSHO Lesser Heat	88
小林古径 KOBAYASHI Kokei	蔬菜 Vegetables	昭和18 1943	紙本	着色 color on paper	額 framed		大雪 TAISETSU Greater Snow	178
小松均 KOMATSU Hitoshi	もや Haze	昭和5 1930	紙本	着色 color on paper	軸 hanging scroll		大雪 TAISETSU Greater Snow	176
近藤浩一路 KONDO Koichiro	三条大橋 Sanjo Bridge	大正4 1925	紙本	墨画 sumi ink on paper		51.8 × 66.4	小満 SHOMAN Lesser Ripening	63

作家名 Artist	作品名 Title	制作年 Date	材質 Medium	技法 Technique	形状 Form	寸法(cm: 高×幅×奥行) Size (cm: h × w × d)	節気 Seasonal Period	掲載頁 page of illustration
近藤悠三 KONDO Yuzo	染付梅花大飾皿 Large Ornamental Dish with Plum Blossoms Design, Blue and White	昭和50 1975	磁器、釉薬 porcelain, glaze	染付 blue underglaze		12.0 × 125.5 × 125.5	雨水 | USUI Rainwater	17
近藤悠三 KONDO Yuzo	柘榴染付壺 Vase with Pomegranate Design, Blue Underglaze	昭和50頃 c. 1975	磁器、釉薬 porcelain, glaze	染付 blue underglaze		34.4 × 32.5 × 32.5	寒露 | KANRO Cold Dew	145
榊原紫峰 SAKAKIBARA Shiho	白蓮図 White Lotus	昭和3頃 c. 1928	絹本 color on silk	着色	軸 hanging scroll	77.0 × 86.0	小暑 | SHOSHO Lesser Heat	92
坂本繁二郎 SAKAMOTO Hanjiro	林檎と馬鈴薯 Apples and Potatoes	昭和15 1940	画布 oil on canvas	油彩	額 framed	45.4 × 53.1	立冬 | RITTO Beginning of Winter	164
坂本繁二郎 SAKAMOTO Hanjiro	母仔馬 Horse with Foal	昭和35 1960	画布 oil on canvas	油彩	額 framed	38.4 × 45.7	清明 | SEIMEI Pure and Clear	45
佐藤潤四郎 SATO Junshiro	クリスタル花器 Crystal Flower Vase	昭和22 1947	クリスタルガラス crystal glass			16.2 × 31.2 × 18.0	夏至 | GESHI Summer Solstice	83
清水南山 SHIMIZU Nanzan	獅子文小箱 Small Casket with Shishi (Imaginary Lion) Design	昭和3 1928	赤銅、銅 akagane, copper	鍛造、象嵌 wrought, inlay		5.3 × 13.6 × 9.8	正月 The New Year	203
清水卯一 SHIMIZU Uichi	柿釉壺 Jar, Reddish-brown Glaze	昭和38 1963	陶器、釉薬 ceramic, glaze			33.1 × 25.1 × 25.1	霜降 | SOKO Frost Falls	155
清水卯一 SHIMIZU Uichi	青瓷大鉢 Large Celadon Bowl	昭和48 1973	青瓷 celadon			16.0 × 40.5 × 40.5	小満 | SHOMAN Lesser Ripening	67
志村ふくみ SHIMURA Fukumi	着物「七夕」 Kimono: Star Festival	昭和35 1960	絹、茜、蘇芳、刈安、藍 silk, madder, sappanwood, kariyasu (miscanthus tinctorius), indigo	紬織 pongee weaving		168.0 × 129.0	立秋 | RISHU Beginning of Autumn	106
志村ふくみ SHIMURA Fukumi	紬織着物「冬樹」 Pongee Kimono: Winter Tree	昭和36 1961	絹糸、蘇芳、莓、藍 silk, bay berry, indigo	紬織 pongee weaving		168.0 × 129.0	小雪 | SHOSETSU Lesser Snow	170
霜鳥之彦 SHIMOTORI Yukihiko	氷屋（於大阪殿前） Summer Teahouse in Front of Taikyokuden	明治37 1904	紙 paper	水彩 watercolor	額 framed	41.2 × 28.5	大暑 | TAISHO Greater Heat	101
霜鳥之彦 SHIMOTORI Yukihiko	麦畑 Field of Wheat	明治38 1905	紙 paper	水彩 watercolor	額 framed	32.5 × 50.7	小満 | SHOMAN Lesser Ripening	68
霜鳥之彦 SHIMOTORI Yukihiko	北野の春 Spring in Kitano	明治39 1906	紙 paper	水彩 watercolor	額 framed	44.4 × 34.3	清明 | SEIMEI Pure and Clear	44
下村良之介 SHIMOMURA Ryonosuke	くるみ Walnut	昭和25 1950	紙本 color on paper	着色 color on paper	額 framed	60.5 × 84.5	寒露 | KANRO Cold Dew	144

作家名 Artist	作品名 Title	制作年 Date	材質 Medium	技法 Technique	形状 Form	寸法(cm：高×幅×奥行) Size (cm: h × w × d)	節気 Seasonal Period	掲載頁 page of illustration
正阿弥勝義 SHOAMI Katsuyoshi	瓢箪に天道虫花瓶 Vase with Gourd and Ladybug Design	明治33 1900	素銅 copper	象嵌（金、銀、赤銅、緋銅） inlay (gold, silver, akagane, hido)		22.0×10.0×10.0	小満 | SHOMAN Lesser Ripening	68
正阿弥勝義 SHOAMI Katsuyoshi	柘榴に蝉飾器 Covered Jar in Shape of Pomegranate and Cicada	明治時代 1868-1912	銅 copper	象嵌（金、赤銅、四分一） inlay (gold, akagane, shibuichi copper alloy)		12.5×11.5×11.0	処暑 | SHOSHO Manageable Heat	118
正阿弥勝義 SHOAMI Katsuyoshi	蓮葉に蛙皿 Dish in Shape of Lotus Leaf with Frog	明治時代 1868-1912	銅 copper	平象嵌（金） inlay (gold)		4.5×13.0×11.0	立夏 | RIKKA Beginning of Summer	62
松風栄一 SHOFU Eiichi	染付花瓶「風雪」 Flower Vase, Blue and White: Wind and Snow	［不詳］ [n. d.]	磁器、釉薬 porcelain, glaze	着色		26.0×30.5×28.5	大雪 | TAISETSU Beginning of Summer	180
白山松哉 SHIRAYAMA Shosai	菊文蒔絵棗 Tea Caddy with Chrysanthemum Design, Maki-e	明治～大正時代 1868-1923	木胎、漆、金 wood, lacquer, gold	蒔絵 maki-e		5.0×6.5×6.5	立秋 | RISSHU Autumn Equinox	134
白山松哉 SHIRAYAMA Shosai	棗「稲」 Tea Caddy: Rice Plant	［不詳］ [n. d.]	木胎、金 wood, lacquer, gold	蒔絵 maki-e		7.8×7.0×7.0	寒露 | KANRO Cold Dew	148
新見虚舟 SHINMI Kyoshu	鮒 Crucian Carps	昭和5 1930	絹本 color on silk	着色	軸 hanging scroll	73.6×71.4	小寒 | SHOKAN Lesser Cold	191
吹田草牧 SUITA Soboku	醍醐寺庭苑 Garden of Daigo-ji Temple	昭和3 1928	絹本 color on silk	着色	二曲一双屏風 two-panels folding screen	168.0×220.0	立冬 | RITTO Beginning of Winter	160
鈴木治 SUZUKI Osamu	雪の中の馬 Horse in the Snow	昭和48 1973	陶器、釉薬 ceramic, glaze			76.5×56.0×29.5	大雪 | TAISETSU Greater Snow	182
鈴木松年 SUZUKI Shonen	名家画帖「画苑」より from Booklet with Famous Artists "Picture Garden"	明治後期 c.1890-1912	絹本 color on silk	着色	画帖（24個） booklet (24 sheets)	20.3×28.3	立秋 | RISSHU Beginning of Autumn	110
鈴田照次 SUZUTA Teruji	木版摺更紗着物「芹花文」 Woodblock Dyed Calico Kimono, Pattern of Japanese Parsely Flower	昭和52 1977	紬絹 silk pongee	木版 woodblock dyed	一着	166.5×115.4	夏至 | GESHI Summer Solstice	85
須田国太郎 SUDA Kunitaro	野菜 Vegetables	昭和15年頃 c.1940	画布 oil on canvas	油彩	額 framed	35.0×60.0	大雪 | TAISETSU Greater Snow	179
須田国太郎 SUDA Kunitaro	夜桜 Cherry Blossoms Reflecting Bonfire	昭和16 1941	画布 oil on canvas	油彩	額 framed	64.5×90.5	春分 | SHUNBUN Spring Equinox	35
須田国太郎 SUDA Kunitaro	動物園 Zoo	昭和28 1953	画布 oil on canvas	油彩	額 framed	60.0×80.0	夏至 | GESHI Summer Solstice	82
精巧山 Seikosan	花見図花瓶 Flower Vase with Cherry Blossoms Viewing Design	明治～大正時代 1868-1926	陶器 ceramic	色絵、金彩 overglaze enamels, gold paint	一対 pair of flower vases	11.9×6.3×6.3 （各 each）	春分 | SHUNBUN Spring Equinox	38

し
す
せ

作家名 Artist	作品名 Title	制作年 Date	材質 Medium	技法 Technique	形状 Form	寸法 (cm; 高×幅×奥行) Size (cm: h × w × d)	節気 Seasonal Period	掲載頁 page of illustration
三代 清風与平 SEIFU Yohei III	奥白磁牡丹文花瓶 *White Porcelain Flower Vase with Peony Design in Relief*	明治後期〜 大正初期 c.1895-1920	磁器、釉薬 porcelain, glaze			41.0 × 29.0 × 29.0	穀雨 | *KOKUU* Grain Rains	51
関根勢之助 SEKINE Seinosuke	六月の声(聲) *Voice of June (Voice)*	昭和39 1964	画布 oil on canvas	油彩	額 framed	194.0 × 130.5	芒種 | *BOSHU* Grain Beards and Seeds	72
芹沢銈介 SERIZAWA Keisuke	型染立樹文着物 *Kimono with Standing Tree Design*	昭和43 1968	木綿紬 cotton pongee	型染 stencil dyed		141.0×64.0 (裄丈: sleeve length)	立冬 | *RITTO* Beginning of Winter	165
高瀬好山 TAKASE Kozan	鯉 自在置物 *Articulated Carp*	明治〜大正時代 1868-1926	四分一 shibuichi copper alloy		自在 articulated figure	11.3 × 32.7 × 11.4	立夏 | *RIKKA* Beginning of Summer	62
高瀬好山 TAKASE Kozan	兜虫 *Beetle*	大正〜昭和初 c.1912-30	鉄 iron		自在 articulated figure	6.1 × 6.9 × 4.0	大暑 | *TAISHO* Greater Heat	100
高瀬好山 TAKASE Kozan	蟷螂 *Mantis*	大正〜昭和初 c.1910-30	鉄 iron		自在 articulated figure	5.5 × 16.6 × 4.7	芒種 | *BOSHU* Grain Beards and Seeds	73
高村豊周 TAKAMURA Toyochika	朱銅花瓶「晩秋」 *Copper Red Flower Vase: Late Autumn*	昭和46 1971	銅 copper			18.5 × 22.8 × 22.8	霜降 | *SOKO* Frost Falls	155
竹内栖鳳 TAKEUCHI Seiho	枯野の狐 *Fox in Desolate Field*	明治30 1897	絹本 color on silk	着色	軸 hanging scroll	145.5 × 87.0	小雪 | *SHOSETSU* Lesser Snow	171
竹内栖鳳 TAKEUCHI Seiho	おぼろ月 *Hazy Moon*	昭和3 1928	紙本 color on paper	着色	軸 hanging scroll	182.0 × 95.0	清明 | *SEIMEI* Pure and Clear	47
竹内栖鳳 TAKEUCHI Seiho	海老 *Mackerels and Prawns*	昭和14 1939	絹本 color on silk	着色	額 framed	67.7 × 87.0	寒露 | *KANRO* Cold Dew	146
竹内栖鳳 TAKEUCHI Seiho	春雪 *Spring Snow*	昭和17 1942	絹本 color on silk	着色	額 framed	74.3 × 90.9	立春 | *RISSHUN* Beginning of Spring	11
竹内碧外 TAKEUCHI Hekigai	青白磁筆架 *Two Brush Rests, Bluish-White Porcelain*	昭和23 1948	磁器、釉薬 porcelain, glaze		筆架(一対) pair of brush rests	【竹: bamboo leaf】 1.4 × 8.0 × 3.1 【蛙: frog】 2.6 × 6.6 × 3.0	立夏 | *RIKKA* Beginning of Summer	62
竹内碧外 TAKEUCHI Hekigai	黄楊蓮香盒 *Incense Stand with Lotus Design, Boxwood*	昭和25 1950	黄楊木、陶器 boxwood, ceramic			4.1 × 18.3 × 11.5	小暑 | *SHOSHO* Lesser Heat	95
田中善之助 TANAKA Zen'nosuke	萩と茶屋 *Bush Clover and a Teahouse*	明治40頃 c.1907	紙 paper	水彩 watercolor	額 framed	28.2 × 36.9	白露 | *HAKURO* White Dew	127
三代 田辺竹雲斎 TANABE Chiku'unsai II	秋立つ *Beginning of Autumn*	昭和60 1985	竹 bamboo			44.5 × 26.5 × 26.5	立秋 | *RISSHU* Beginning of Autumn	112
谷角日沙春 TANIKADO Hisaharu	葉ぼたんと現代少女 *A Modern Girl with Ornamental Kale*	昭和24 1949	絹本 color on silk	着色 color	軸 hanging scroll	146.5 × 51.8	小寒 | *SHOKAN* Lesser Cold	194

Section markers in margin: せ, そ, た

作家名 Artist	作品名 Title	制作年 Date	材質 Medium	技法 Technique	形状 Form	寸法 (cm: 高 h × 幅 w × 奥行 d) Size	節気 Seasonal Period	掲載頁 page of illustration
三代 田畑喜八 TABATA Kihachi III	友禅菊華文振袖 Long-sleeved Kimono with Chrysanthemum Design	大正末頃 c. 1925	絹 silk	友禅 yuzen dyed		180.0 × 132.0	寒露 | KANRO Cold Dew	141
玉村方久斗 TAMAMURA Hokuto	休日 Holiday	昭和6 1931	紙本 color on paper	着色	額 framed	60.0 × 60.0	穀雨 | KOKU Grain Rains	52
千種掃雲 CHIGUSA Soun	つれづれの日 A Tedious Day	明治42 1909	絹本 color on silk	着色	額 framed	102.5 × 72.5	大寒 | DAIKAN Greater Cold	197
千種掃雲 CHIGUSA Soun	下鴨神社夏越神事 Summer Shinto Ritual at Shimogamo-jinja Shrine	[不詳] [n.d.]	絹本 color on silk	着色	軸 hanging scroll	123.0 × 36.5	夏至 | GESHI Summer Solstice	84
中堂憲一 CHUDO Ken'ichi	能の女 井筒 Female Figure of Nob Play "Izutsu"	平成2 1990	布 cloth	型染 stencil dyed	額 framed	72.0 × 59.7	秋分 | SHUBUN Autumn Equinox	137
二十代 椎朱楊成 TSUISHU Yozei XX	乾漆木蓮図硯箱 Inkstone Box with Mulan Magnolia Design, Kanshitsu Technique	大正6 1917	木胎、漆、金、貝 wood, lacquer, gold, lead, shell	乾漆、螺鈿 dry lacquer, raden inlay		4.5 × 22.5 × 21.0	啓蟄 | KEICHITSU Insects Awaken	29
二十代 椎朱楊成 TSUISHU Yozei XX	紅花緑葉獅子香盆 Tray with Red Flowers, Green Leaf and Shishi (Imaginary Lion) Design	大正8 1919	木、漆 wood, lacquer	彫漆 carved lacquer		3.5 × 25.8 × 25.8	正月 The New Year	203
都路華香 TSUJI Kako	白雲紅樹 White Clouds over Red Leaves	大正3頃 c. 1914	絹本 color on silk	着色	軸 hanging scroll	127.1 × 56.5	立冬 | RITTO Beginning of Winter	162
土田麦僊 TSUCHIDA Bakusen	鮭 Dish of Salmon	大正14 1924	絹本 color on silk	着色	軸 hanging scroll	39.0 × 50.0	立春 | RISSHUN Beginning of Spring	13
土田麦僊 TSUCHIDA Bakusen	朝顔 Morning Glories	昭和3 1928	紙本 color on paper	着色	二曲一双屏風 pair of two-panels folding screens	180.0 × 200.0 (各: each)	処暑 | SHOSHO Manageable Heat	114
デイヴィッド・ホックニー David HOCKNEY	Kyoto 24 April 1993	平成5 1993	紙 paper	リトグラフ lithograph	額 framed	41.1 × 161.8	穀雨 | KOKU Grain Rains	53
寺島紫明 TERASHIMA Shimei	彼岸 Prayer	昭和21 1946	絹本 color on silk	着色	額 framed	128.5 × 67.3	春分 | SHUNBUN Spring Equinox	31
堂本印象 DOMOTO Insho	冬朝 Winter Morning	昭和7 1932	絹本 color on silk	着色	額 framed	168.0 × 187.0	大雪 | TAISETSU Greater Snow	174
堂本尚郎 DOMOTO Hisao	蓮池 Lotus Pond	平成17 2005	画布 oil on canvas	油彩	額 framed	80.0 × 80.0	小暑 | SHOSHO Lesser Heat	93
徳岡神泉 TOKUOKA Shinsen	罌粟 Poppies	昭和8 1933	紙本 color on paper	着色	額 framed	172.3 × 152.5	立夏 | RIKKA Beginning of Summer	61

作家名 Artist	作品名 Title	制作年 Date	材質 Medium	技法 Technique	形状 Form	寸法 (cm: 高×幅×奥行) Size (cm. h × w × d)	節気 Seasonal Period	掲載頁 page of illustration
な 滑川悠助 NAMIKAWA Sosuke	藤図花瓶 Vase with Wisteria Design	明治時代 1868-1910	金属・七宝 metal, glaze	無線・有線七宝 non-wired and wired cloisonné		30.6 × 12.6 × 12.6	立夏 RIKKA Beginning of Summer	58
に 西川實 NISHIKAWA Minoru	潮流 Spring Tide	昭和42 1967	陶器・釉薬 ceramic, glaze			43.0 × 37.0 × 37.0	春分 SHUNBUN Spring Equinox	32
西嶋武司 NISHIJIMA Takeshi	麦秋 Wheat Harvest	昭和38 1963	綿 cotton	染 dyed	二曲一隻屏風 two-panels folding screen	169.0 × 184.8	小満 SHOMAN Lesser Ripening	69
西村五雲 NISHIMURA Goun	閑日 After Noon	昭和6 1931	絹本 color on silk	着彩	軸 hanging scroll	56.0 × 71.5	立秋 RISSHU Beginning of Autumn	110
西村五雲 NISHIMURA Goun	鮮魚 Fresh Fish	c.1931 昭和6頃	絹本 color on silk	着彩	軸 hanging scroll	56.7 × 64.8	清明 SEIMEI Pure and Clear	46
西村五雲 NISHIMURA Goun	山の幸川の幸 Bounty of the Mountains and River	昭和13 1938	絹本 color on silk	着彩	軸 hanging scroll	53.2 × 62.8	小満 SHOMAN Lesser Ripening	64
八世 西村彦兵衛（象彦）NISHIMURA Hikobei VIII (Zohiko)	羽衣蒔絵料紙硯箱 Writing Paper Box and Inkstone Box with Hagoromo (Robe of Feathers) Design, Maki-e (Zohiko)	明治末〜昭和初 c.1910-30	木、漆、金 wood, lacquer, gold	蒔絵 maki-e		【料紙箱：writing paper box】15.0 × 35.5 × 43.5 【硯箱：inkstone box】4.8 × 24.0 × 26.5	立春 RISSHUN Beginning of Spring	10
の 野島康三 NOJIMA Yasuzo	［題名不詳］[Title Unknown]	昭和5 1930		ブロムオイル・プリント bromoil print	軸 hanging scroll	26.5 × 40.6	芒種 BOSHU Grain Beards and Seeds	77
野島康三 NOJIMA Yasuzo	枇杷 Loquats	昭和5 1930		ブロムオイル・プリント bromoil print		23.3 × 39.8	芒種 BOSHU Grain Beards and Seeds	77
野島康三 NOJIMA Yasuzo	庭の隅所見 A View of the Garden Corner	昭和5 1930		ブロムオイル・プリント bromoil print		30.2 × 38.8	小暑 SHOSHO Manageable Heat	113
野島康三 NOJIMA Yasuzo	静物 Still Life	昭和17 1942		ゼラチン・シルバー・プリント gelatin silver print		55.3 × 45.6	小寒 SHOKAN Lesser Cold	193
野島康三 NOJIMA Yasuzo	雪 Snow	昭和17 1942		ゼラチン・シルバー・プリント gelatin silver print		55.5 × 45.5	大雪 TAISETSU Greater Snow	181
野島康三 NOJIMA Yasuzo	チューリップ Tulips	昭和15 1940		ゼラチン・シルバー・プリント gelatin silver print		54.2 × 44.9	処暑 SHOSHO Manageable Heat	27
野島康三 NOJIMA Yasuzo	初秋 Early Autumn	昭和5 1930		ブロムオイル・プリント bromoil print		27.3 × 39.2	処暑 SHOSHO Manageable Heat	113
野長瀬晩花 NONAGASE Banka	遅日 Long Spring Day	大正9頃 c.1920	絹本 color on silk	着色	軸 hanging scroll	130.6 × 42.1	啓蟄 KEICHITSU Insects Awaken	25
は バーナード・リーチ Bernard LEACH	楽焼大皿［兎］ Large Raku Ware Dish: Rabbit	大正9 1920	陶器、釉薬 ceramic, glaze			6.5 × 35.5 × 35.5	小雪 SHOSETSU Lesser Snow	167

作家名 Artist	作品名 Title	制作年 Date	材質 Medium	技法 Technique	形状 Form	寸法 (cm; 高×幅×奥行) Size (cm; h × w × d)	節気 Seasonal Period	掲載頁 page of illustration
ひ 平石晃祥 HIRAISHI Kosho	八仙花 *Hydrangea*	昭和59 1984	木、漆 wood, lacquer			17.0 × 17.5 × 37.0	芒種 | *BOSHU* Grain Beards and Seeds	74
ふ 深見陶治 FUKAMI Toji	清晨 *Cool Morning*	昭和59 1984	磁器、釉薬 porcelain, glaze			42.0 × 34.0 × 37.0	処暑 | *SHOSHO* Manageable Heat	117
福田平八郎 FUKUDA Heihachiro	清晨 *Cool Morning*	昭和10 1935	絹本 color on silk	着色	軸 hanging scroll	141.5 × 51.0	処暑 | *SHOSHO* Manageable Heat	116
福田平八郎 FUKUDA Heihachiro	竹 *Bamboo*	昭和17 1942	紙本 color on paper	着色	額 framed	55.2 × 72.0	立夏 | *RIKKA* Beginning of Summer	60
福元しづ子 FUKUMOTO Shihoko	夏着尺「ともしび」 *Summer Kimono Cloth, Light*	平成16 2004	夏山絹 silk	藍染、絞染 indigo dyed, tie dyed	軸 hanging scroll	1450.0 × 38.0	芒種 | *BOSHU* Grain Beards and Seeds	73
藤井達吉 FUJII Tatsukichi	七宝あざみ小皿 *Cloisonné Small Dishes With Thistle Design*	大正5-12 1916-23	銅、釉薬 copper, glaze	打ち出し、七宝 repoussé, cloisonné	皿4点 4 dishes	1.8 × 11.2 × 11.2 (各: each)	清明 | *SEIMEI* Pure and Clear	48
藤井達吉 FUJII Tatsukichi	橘文菓子器 *Sweets Bowl with Tachibana Orange Design*	大正5-12 1916-23	木 wood	金彩 gold paint		5.5 × 18.0 × 18.0	夏至 | *GESHI* Summer Solstice	80
藤井達吉 FUJII Tatsukichi	鶏頭文衣箱 *Clothes Tray with Cockscomb Design*	[不詳] [n.d.]	木、鉛 wood, lead	象嵌、着色 inlay, hand colored		10.0 × 55.0 × 38.5	白露 | *HAKURO* White Dew	128
藤田嗣平 FUJITA Kyohei	飾筥「早春」 *Decorative Box: Early Spring*	昭和64 1984	ガラス glass			15.8 × 30.1 × 30.1	雨水 | *USUI* Rainwater	20
藤田嗣平 FUJITA Kyohei	飾筥「醍醐」 *Decorative Box: Daigo*	平成7頃 c.1995	ガラス glass			20.0 × 29.2 × 28.0	清明 | *SEIMEI* Pure and Clear	42
藤本能道 FUJIMOTO Yoshimichi	色絵銀彩合歓双雀図筥 *Box with a Pair of Sparrows and Silk Tree Leaves Design, Overglaze Enamels and Silver*	昭和57 1982	磁器、釉薬 porcelain, glaze	色絵銀彩 overglaze enamels, silver paint		5.5 × 32.0 × 32.0	小暑 | *SHOSHO* Lesser Heat	95
不動立山 FUDO Ritsuzan	夕立 *Shower*	昭和5 1930	絹本 color on silk	着色	額 framed	233.5 × 174.8	小暑 | *SHOSHO* Lesser Heat	94
船越春眠 FUNAKOSHI Shunmin	柿形香盒 *Kaki-shaped Incense Case*	昭和11 1936	銅 copper	鋳造 casting		1.8 × 6.8 × 6.8	霜降 | *SOKO* Frost Falls	154
ポール・カポニグロ Paul CAPONIGRO	向日葵 *Sunflower*	昭和40 1965		ゼラチン・シルバー・プリント gelatin silver print		27.1 × 25.9	立秋 | *RISSHU* Beginning of Autumn	108
ほ 堀内正和 HORIUCHI Masakazu	エヴァからもらった大きなリンゴ *Large Apple from Eva*	昭和41 1966	合金、大理石 alloy, marble			18.0 × 30.0 × 25.0	立冬 | *RITTO* Beginning of Winter	164

作家名 Artist	作品名 Title	制作年 Date	材質 Medium	技法 Technique	形状 Form	寸法 (cm: 高×幅×奥行) Size (cm: h × w × d)	節気 Seasonal Period	掲載頁 page of illustration
増田三男 MASUDA Mitsuo	銀象嵌鴫文箱 Box with Snipes Design, Silver Inlay	昭和42 1967	鉄、銀 iron, silver	鍛造、象嵌 wrought, inlay		10.0 × 17.0 × 9.0	白露 | HAKURO White Dew	130
松田権六 MATSUDA Gonroku	蒔絵箱「赤とんぼ」 Casket with Red Dragonflies Design, Maki-e	昭和44 1969	木胎、金、貝 wood, gold, mother-of-pearl	蒔絵、螺鈿 maki-e, raden inlay		11.3 × 15.5 × 27.5	処暑 | SHOSHO Manageable Heat	119
松原直子 MATSUBARA Naoko	七夕祭(竹取物語より) Star Festival from "The Tale of the Bamboo Cutter"	昭和40 1965	紙 paper	木版 woodblock print	額 framed	46.5 × 52.0	小暑 | SHOSHO Lesser Heat	88
真野紀太郎 MANO Kitaro	薔薇 Roses	昭和36 1941	紙 paper	水彩 watercolor	額 framed	57.2 × 77.7	小満 | SHOMAN Lesser Ripening	66
丸岡比呂史 MARUOKA Hiroshi	金魚 Goldfish	大正末 c. 1925	絹本 color on silk	着色	軸 hanging scroll	39.5 × 59.6	大暑 | TAISHO Greater Heat	99
三浦景生 MIURA Kageo	布象嵌「末摘花」 Cloth Inlay: Suetsumuhana (Safflower)	昭和47 1972	麻 hemp	染、布象嵌 dyed, cloth inlay	二曲一隻屏風 two-panels folding screen	166.2 × 181.6	小暑 | SHOSHO Lesser Heat	91
二代 三木表悦 MIKI Hyoetsu II	薔薇と人物 Rose and Figures	昭和7頃 c. 1932	木、漆 wood, lacquer			2.3 × 44.7 × 44.7	小満 | SHOMAN Lesser Ripening	66
水越松南 MIZUKOSHI Shonan	一陽来復 Winter Ends and Spring Arrives	昭和23 1948	絹本 color on silk	着色	軸 hanging scroll	60.5 × 73.0	正月 | TOJI The New Year	202
三谷十糸子 MITANI Toshiko	露店 Street Stall	昭和4 1929	絹本 color on silk	着色	二曲一隻屏風 two-panels folding screen	165.0 × 168.0	冬至 | TOJI Winter Solstice	185
三代 宮永東山 (宮永理吉) MIYANAGA Tozan III (MIYANAGA Rikichi)	海 Ocean	昭和48 1973	磁器、釉薬 porcelain, glaze			29.5 × 28.0 × 29.0	大暑 | TAISHO Greater Heat	102
三輪良平 MIWA Ryohei	八朔 Gion's Hassaku (The First Day of the Eighth Month of the Ancient Japanese Calendar)	平成15 2003	紙本 color on paper	着色	額 framed	191.0 × 155.0	大暑 | TAISHO Greater Heat	97
村上華岳 MURAKAMI Kagaku	田植の頃 Season of Rice Planting	明治45 1912	紙本 color on paper	着色	二曲一隻屏風 two-panels folding screen	157.5 × 191.0	小満 | SHOMAN Lesser Ripening	63
村上華岳 MURAKAMI Kagaku	夜桜之図 Evening Scene of Cherry Blossoms Viewing	大正2 1913	絹本 color on silk	着色	二曲一隻屏風 two-panels folding screen	142.8 × 160.0	春分 | SHUNBUN Spring Equinox	36
村上華岳 MURAKAMI Kagaku	鰈 Flatfish	大正11 1922	絹本 color on silk	着色	軸 hanging scroll	37.5 × 51.0	春分 | SHUNBUN Spring Equinox	32
村上華岳 MURAKAMI Kagaku	観音之図(聖蓮華) Avalokitesvara (The Sacred Lotus)	昭和5 1930	紙本 paper	淡彩 light color on paper	軸 hanging scroll	132.0 × 31.3	啓蟄 | KEICHITSU Insects Awaken	28

作家名 Artist	作品名 Title	制作年 Date	材質 Medium	技法 Technique	形状 Form	寸法 (cm: 高×幅×奥行) Size (cm: h × w × d)	節気 Seasonal Period	掲載頁 page of illustration
4 吉田白嶺、藤井達吉 YOSHIDA Hakurei, FUJII Tatsukichi	上代雛と雛屏風 *Jodai-bina Dolls and Folding Screen*	[不詳] [n.d.]	木 wood	着色 colored		【男雛】obina: 15.0 × 10.0 × 7.0 【女雛】mebina: 15.0 × 8.5 × 8.0 【台】stage: 5.8 × 28.7 × 18.0 【屏風】folding screen: 0.8 × 73.2 × 30.5	雨水 | USUI Rainwater	16
吉原治良 YOSHIHARA Jiro	朝顔と海産物 *Morning Glories and Marine Products*	昭和3 1928	画布 oil on canvas	油彩	額 framed	80.3 × 100.0	処暑 | SHOSHO Manageable Heat	115
5 十五代 樂吉左衞門 RAKU Kichizaemon XV	萩焼茶碗「香雪」 *Hagi Ware Teabowl: Snow Scene Viewing*	平成27 2015	陶器、釉薬 ceramic, glaze			9.0 × 17.0 × 15.0	大雪 | TAISETSU Greater Snow	180
3 六角紫水 ROKKAKU Shisui	菊蝶文香合 *Incense Case with Chrysanthemum and Butterfly Design*	[不詳] [n.d.]	木、漆、金、銀 wood, lacquer, gold, silver	蒔絵 maki-e		2.3 × 7.5 × 7.5	寒露 | KANRO Cold Dew	148
[不詳] [Unknown]	龍自在置物 *Dragon, Articulated Ornament*	江戸末~ 明治時代 c. 1860-1912	鉄 iron			10.9 × 27.0 × 7.5	啓蟄 | KEICHITSU Insects Awaken	28
[不詳] [Unknown]	清水寺図額 *View of Kiyomizu-dera Temple*	明治時代 1868-1912	絹 silk	刺繡 embroidery	額 framed	22.0 × 30.5	清明 | SEIMI Pure and Clear	44
[不詳] [Unknown]	紅葉・雪中之景図 *Scenes of Red Leaves and Snow*	明治11-44 1879-1911	天鵞絨 velvet	友禅 yuzen dyed		65.0 × 59.0	大雪 | TAISETSU Greater Snow	176
[不詳] [Unknown]	藤に孔雀図刺繡蝶掛 *Tapestry with Peacock and Paben with Wisteria Design*	明治38頃 c. 1905	絹 silk	刺繡 embroidery		181.0 × 249.0	立夏 | RIKKA Beginning of Summer	58

[展覧会情報]

本書は、左記展覧会の関連書籍として刊行された。
This book was edited and published on the occasion of the following exhibition.

京都国立近代美術館所蔵作品による｜From MoMAK Collection

京のくらし──二十四節気を愉しむ
Life in Kyoto ──Arts in Seasonal Delight

会期　二〇二〇年七月二十三日（木・祝）─九月二十二日（火・祝）
会場　京都国立近代美術館
主催　京都国立近代美術館、NHK京都放送局、KBS京都、京都新聞

23 July – 22 September, 2020
The National Museum of Modern Art, Kyoto (MoMAK)

──

筧 菜奈子
一九八六年生まれ。現代美術・装飾史研究。二〇一二年東京藝術大学美術学部芸術学科卒業。二〇一八年京都大学大学院人間・環境学研究科博士後期課程終了。博士（人間・環境学）。二〇二〇年より東海大学教養学部芸術学科特任講師。

KAKEI Nanako
Born in 1986, Contemporary Art and Decoration history researcher in Japan. Graduated from Tokyo University of the Arts, Department of Aesthetics and Art History, 2011. Ph.D. from Kyoto University, Graduate School of Human and Environmental Studies, 2018. From 2020, Lecturer, Tokai University, Department of Liberal Arts.

[凡例]

・作品ページは、展覧会に関連した十二の章と一つの別章で構成される。
・巻末の作品データは、原則として美術館より提供されたデータに基づき、次の順に記した。
・作家名／作品名／制作年／材質・技法／形状・寸法／展覧会による節気区分／図版掲載ページ
・各章の解説および作品解説は、筧菜奈子が執筆した。
・掲載作品のうち、展覧会会場で展示されていないものがある。
・掲載作品の順番は展覧会会場の展示順と一致しない。
・すべての作品は、京都国立近代美術館所蔵である。

[Explanatory Notes]

・The pages on the artworks are composed of twelve chapters related to the exhibition and one supplementary chapter.
・The data on the artworks are based on information provided by MoMAK in the following order.
・Artist / Title / Date / Medium / Technique / Form / Size / Seasonal Period of Exhibition Display / Page presented in this book.
・Chapter and artwork descriptions were written by Kakei Nanako.
・Some of the artworks presented in this book are not exhibited.
・The order of the artworks in this book does not correspond to the order in the exhibition.
・All of the artworks belong to the Collection of The National Museum of Modern Art, Kyoto.

本書は、展覧会「京(みやこ)のくらしーー二十四節気を愉しむ」展の関連書籍として刊行されました。
This book was edited and published on the occasion of the exhibition 'Life in Kyoto — Arts in Seasonal Delight'.

京都国立近代美術館所蔵作品にみる｜From MoMAK Collection

京(みやこ)のくらしーー二十四節気を愉しむ
Life in Kyoto —— Arts in Seasonal Delight

編著：京都国立近代美術館＋筧菜奈子
Edited by The National Museum of Modern Art, Kyoto + KAKEI Nanako

執筆：筧菜奈子、池田祐子（京都国立近代美術館）
Text: KAKEI Nanako, IKEDA Yuko

編集：池田祐子、古屋歴（青幻舎）
Editors: IKEDA Yuko, FURUYA Ayumi (Seigensha Art Publishing, Inc.)

協力：平井啓修、高見澤なごみ（京都国立近代美術館）
Editorial Assistants: HIRAI Yoshinobu, TAKAMISAWA Nagomi (MoMAK)

デザイン：木村幸央
Design: KIMURA Yukio

翻訳：Beth Cary
Translation: Beth CARY

撮影：木村羊一（p.17-1, p.38-3, p.58-3, p.100-3, p.111-1, p.111-4, p.148-4, p.154-2, p.198-2, p.204-2, p.204-3）、
Photo: KIMURA Yoichi (p.17-1, p.38-3, p.58-3, p.100-3, p.111-1, p.111-4, p.148-4, p.154-2, p.198-2, p.204-2, p.204-3),
今村裕司、四方邦煕
IMAMURA Yuji, SHIKATA Kunihiro
その他画像提供：京都国立近代美術館
Others MoMAK

p.96　日本の夏｜ハンナ・ヘーヒ
Summer in Japan | Hannah HÖCH
© VG BILD-KUNST, Bonn & JASPAR, Tokyo, 2020 G2262

p.117　楽焼葡萄文花入｜バーナード・リーチ
Vase with Grape and Vine Leaf Design, Raku Ware | Bernard LEACH

p.167　楽焼大皿［兎］｜バーナード・リーチ
Large Raku Ware Dish: Rabbit | Bernard LEACH
© The Bernard Leach Family, All rights reserved, DACS & JASPAR 2020 G2262

p.203　獅子頭｜熊谷守一
Head of Shishi (A Mask for Dance Dedicated to Gods) | KUMAGAI Morikazu
© Kaya Kumagai

発行者：安田英樹
発行所：株式会社青幻舎
〒604-8136　京都市中京区梅忠町9-1
Tel 075-252-6766
Fax 075-252-6770
www.seigensha.com

Published by Seigensha Art Publishing, inc.
9-1, Umetada-cho, Nakagyo-ku, Kyoto, 604-8136

印刷・製本：株式会社ライブアートブックス
Printing and Binding: Live Art Books Inc.

発行日：二〇二〇年七月二十三日　初版発行
First Edition July 23, 2020

ISBN978-4-86152-794-4 C0070

Printed in Japan

『京のくらし──二十四節気を愉しむ』正誤一覧

本書に誤りがありました。下記、お詫びして訂正いたします。

作品掲載頁／作品リスト頁	作品	訂正箇所	正	誤
13／230	鮭	年代	大正13	大正14
63／235	田植の頃	技法	絹本、着色 color on silk	紙本、着色 color on paper
65／220	水神貴船奥宮	作家名 （解説文・クレジット）	宇田荻邨	宇田荻邨
66／235	薔薇	年代	昭和16	昭和36
86		解説文	三十三基の山鉾巡行 the procession of thirty-three gorgeously decorated floats.	二十三基の山鉾巡業 the procession of twenty-three gorgeously decorated floats.
121／231	色絵飾筥	年代	1941	1970